THE PSYCHOLOGY OF JESUS

THE PSYCHOLOGY OF JESUS

THE DYNAMICS OF CHRISTIAN WHOLENESS

DAVID McKENNA

WORD BOOKS
PUBLISHER
WACO, TEXAS

A DIVISION OF
WORD, INCORPORATED

To my friends and critics—
the students
of
Seattle Pacific University

CONTENTS

THE
PSYCHOLOGY
OF
JESUS

PREFACE

CHRISTIAN SCHOLARS must take responsibility for integrating faith and learning. Otherwise, generations of Christians will learn to accommodate their beliefs to secular values, humanistic theories, and unresolved moral issues.

After twenty years as a teacher and administrator in Christian higher education, I am convinced that the faith and learning questions in the behavioral sciences will be the pivots upon which the quality of our witness turns in the last quarter of the twentieth century. Therefore, without pretending to be a scholar in either psychology or theology, I have tried to present a "DEW-Line" report on the psychology of Jesus. I hope it will stimulate Christian scholars in secular as well as Christian colleges and universities to come to grips with the moral issues in their fields that also concern their faith. Origen, who might be considered the father of Christian scholarship, led the way for this mission when he confronted pagan philosophies with Christianity in the Forum at Alexandria. Secular scholarship still awaits the challenge of Christianity, and the Christian community desperately needs ethical guidelines for the multiplying moral dilemmas of our age.

Motivation for this study came from a "Confrontation" series that I presented in chapel at Seattle Pacific University. The response of the faculty and students suggested that the "nerve center" of the teaching-learning process had been touched. Therefore, the Board of Trustees granted me a presidential sabbatical in order to finish the book. If there is grit between the pages, it is the white sands of Makaha Beach in Hawaii. My family swam while I wrote, and then when the creative juices stopped flowing, I recharged them by looking at the bottom of the Pacific Ocean through a diving mask.

So many people had a part in this book that I cannot name them all.

Janet, my wife, who has mastered the art of loving motivation;

Doug and Deb, our older children, who are unawed critics of a university president;

Sue and Rob, our second set, who still wonder what Daddy's going to be when he grows up;

Cec Tindall, my executive assistant, and Joyce King, administrative secretary, who have learned to use the heat in the kitchen to become gourmets of the president's office;

Pat, my sister, who failed to give me credit in her doctoral thesis.

For each of them, I only ask that they might join me in seeking the personal wholeness that Jesus promises to us. For the students who read the book, my hope is that they will be stimulated to Christian scholarship and take up the study where I have fallen short.

DAVID L. MCKENNA
Seattle, Washington

Part One

THE QUESTION

*"But what about you—
who do you say that I am?"*
Mark 8:29

Chapter One

WHO IS JESUS?

CHRISTIAN FAITH pivots on a person—Jesus of Nazareth. If Jesus is fully God and fully man as he claimed to be, then all human history is subject to his authority. As the Son of God, he claimed to be our Lord; as the Son of Man, he claimed to be our Model; and as fully God and fully man, he claimed to be our Redeemer.

When the case of Christianity is presented in the secular world, the authority of Jesus as Lord and Redeemer carries the weight of the argument. Contemporary men and women, however, are confronting the prospects of a dehumanized society in which the meaning of persons and interpersonal relationships is becoming a matter of survival. In response, we cannot forget that Jesus' claim to be the Son of Man holds equal authority in the Christian portfolio. If Jesus was a real and complete man who participated fully in the human expe-

13

rience, then he must be our Model and our hope. Anything less and the case for Christianity is dismissed.

THE CHRISTOLOGICAL QUESTION

In theology, the relationship between the divinity and the humanity of Jesus is called *the christological question.* Jesus himself focused the issue when he asked the disciples, "Who are men saying that I am?" (Mark 8:27). Four different answers came back—an ascetic like John the Baptist, a visionary like Elijah, a weeper like Jeremiah, and a thunderer like one of the prophets. Not satisfied, Jesus pressed further, "But what about you—who do you say that I am?" (Mark 8:29). In a flash of insight, Peter answered, "You are [God's] Christ!" (Mark 8:29).

Since that time, the christological controversy has never ceased. Some confess with Peter that Jesus Christ is the Son of the living God:

I believe in God the Father Almighty, Maker of heaven and earth;
And in Jesus Christ his only Son our Lord.

(The Apostle's Creed)

Others have denied his deity, and still others have tipped the scale toward his humanity until he has become a brother but not a Savior. Whatever the response, there is no neutral ground when we confront the question of the person of Jesus Christ.

JESUS OF THE ARTISTS

Each of us tends to remake Jesus in our own image. He has been colored, culturized, and corrupted by each generation. Contemporary posters depicting Jesus the revolutionary are no more sacrilegious than the treatment he has received from the chisels of sculptors, the brushes of artists, and the pens of authors for the past two thousand years. The gaunt, depressed, bleeding Jesus of the medieval artist stands in sharp relief against the soft and pretty head painted by Sallman or the surrealistic impressions of Dali. Likewise, the tragic but redemptive Christ-figure in Dostoevski's novels can hardly be identified with the frustrated lover of Mary Magdalene in Kazantzakis's *The Last Temptation of Christ*.

Dramatists further extended artistic license when they put Jesus on the stage. Who would believe that the hushed figure on the center cross in the Passion Play at Oberammergau is the same slick rock-and-roller of *Jesus Christ, Superstar* or the raucous clown of *Godspell* in his Superman T-shirt? In answer to the eternal question "Who do you say that I am?" touristy spectators at the Passion Play become awe-struck participants in the death of the Son of God. A dissonant chord is heard in *Superstar*. Mary Magdalene, in torch-singer style, belts out the rejoinder that Jesus is just a man like so many other men she's known. *Godspell* provokes quite a different answer, particularly among Christians. When the play was produced at a Christian college, telephones rang in protest. Some discriminating constituents objected to the finale, in which the lifeless body of Jesus is carried off-stage without a specific promise of the resurrection. Most of the callers, however, were incensed at the costuming of Jesus— not the overpainted clown-face or the Superman T-shirt, but the broken-down tennis shoes. Illustrating the case in point, Christians can handle a silly or a super-Jesus, but we cannot accept a God who stands in the scuffed humanity of our tennis shoes.

Artists, novelists, and playwrights are expected to exercise vivid imagination in their creations. Because they traffic in symbols, we can indulge the differences and most of the extremes in their portrayals of Jesus. More, however, is expected of theologians and psychologists. Theologians have

16

access to documentary evidence and historical facts as the basis for their search. Psychologists have complementary theories and research techniques for descriptive studies of persons. Their work should reflect the discipline of scholarly study and the accuracy of proven results.

JESUS OF THE THEOLOGIANS

Regretfully, theologians have traded schismatic controversy for the artists' imagination in their responses to the christological question. As soon as the early Christian church began to formulate doctrine, the theological fathers split over the divine and human natures of Jesus. In the Aryan controversy, for example, the test of orthodoxy turned upon an iota in the Greek word used to describe Jesus' nature. Arius, a scholar from Alexandria, was banished from the empire by Constantine because he refused to sign the Nicene Creed which included the word *homoousian*—making Jesus of one essence with the Father.

Under church control and political sanction, an orthodox view of Jesus as Son of God and Son of man prevailed through the Reformation. Then, with the coming of the eighteenth-century Enlightenment, German rationalism refired the issue. With all the "givens" of human knowledge up for grabs, theologians donned the mental dress of devil's advocates and asked, "Can anything good come out of Nazareth?" (John 1:46). As vigorously as the church had defended the deity of Christ, the new critics repudiated his claims with such invectives as "myth, impostor, psychotic." [1] Further fuel was added to the controversy by the introduction of a new scientific spirit in theology. Through a process known as literary, or "higher," criticism of the Scriptures, the Gospels were shorn of their mythical, cultural, and sentimental elements. Jesus was restored "historically" as ". . . a great man, a profound teacher, a splendid example, a heroic martyr, but merely a product of his times, a mere man with all of the limitations of his period." [2]

Contemporary theologians have not let the question rest. Karl Barth's "wholly transcendent God," Paul Tillich's "new Being," Rudolf Bultmann's "demythology," and Thomas Altizer's "Christian atheism" are all variations on a theme that directly involves the person of Jesus Christ. Altizer, a leader in the "Death of God" movement, revealed the motive of his theological colleagues: "A truly contemporary Christ cannot become present to us until we ourselves have died to every shadow and fragment of his transcendent image." [3]

JESUS OF THE PSYCHOLOGISTS

Jesus has been an enigma to psychologists. As a scientific discipline, psychology had its formal beginnings in Germany during the Enlightenment. Its roots were intertwined with theology and philosophy as well as with medicine. In its infancy, scholars were thoroughly enamored with the far-reaching claims of the new science. Not only did they plan to describe human personality, but they looked forward to advanced research that would lead to the prediction and control of human behavior. If then extended to its logical conclusion, psychological theory promised a scientific philosophy of life which would be a substitute for mythical religion. Perhaps this is why the personality of Jesus was subjected to analysis *in absentia* by German scholars. With just enough information to be dangerous, theologians made Jesus a case study in order to bolster their claim that he was an impostor.

A theologian named David Strauss, using psychological terms, indicted Jesus as a twisted fanatic whose ideas of the messianic kingdom bordered on insanity. By comparison, Friedrich Nietzsche was mild in his later denunciation of Jesus' teaching as morbid and immature. But the attacks peaked with Margaret Washburn's trumpeted conclusion: "After a fair and impartial reading of the Gospels, the world must be convinced that Jesus was not divine, but insane." [4] Presumably, the file on the case was then locked by Charles Binet-Sanglé, a physician-psychiatrist, who diagnosed the agony of Jesus in the Garden of Gethsemane as a vasomotor attack brought on by the chill of the night air. From the sweat, groaning, and depression of the experience, Binet-Sanglé concluded, "Nothing further is required for declaring that the founder of the Christian religion was a psychic degenerate." [5]

Albert Schweitzer entered the fray with his doctoral dissertation, *The Psychiatric Study of Jesus*. He gathered facts against Jesus, weighed arguments of the critics, and pronounced judgment upon their conclusions. According to Schweitzer's research, the psychopathological diagnosis of Jesus' personality was faulty because: (1) the evidence was not based on historical material; (2) the investigators did not consider the thought and culture of Jesus' time; (3) the case was constructed with hypothetical symptoms; and (4) the only symptoms that could be discussed from a historical and psychiatric point of view, namely, Jesus' high estimate of himself and perhaps his hallucination at the time of baptism, fell far short of proving the existence of mental illness.

Schweitzer's arguments were conclusive. Since then, the question of the psychic health of Jesus has not surfaced with the support of theological or psychological scholars. A novelist, Hugh Schonfield, threw a pebble into the pond in 1968 with a best-seller called *The Passover Plot*. Consistent with his commercial motive, he quickly followed with *The Jesus Party*.[6] To him, Jesus was an egotist who capitalized on the messianic fervor of his day. Colluding with his disciples, he engineered the crucifixion and resurrection through the clever use of drugs. Schonfield's books may have given him visibility on television talk shows and an extra laugh on the way to the bank, but in the scholarly community where it counts he was ignored. At best, *The Passover Plot* will be remembered as a B-rated film that played in second-run theaters—ironically, as a double feature with *Eternal Sunrise.*

While Schweitzer settled the issue of the psychic health of Jesus, he side-stepped the christological question by discussing the divine-human nature of Jesus as symbol rather than fact. The Jesus of Albert Schweitzer was a strong-willed idealist whose victory was in his death rather than in his Resurrection. Schweitzer wrote:

> In the knowledge that he is the coming son of man, Jesus lays hold of the wheel of the world to set it moving on that last revolution which is to bring all ordinary history to a close. It refuses to turn, and he throws himself upon it. Then it does turn and crushes him. Instead of bringing in the eschatological conditions, he has destroyed them. The wheel rolls onward, and the mangled body of the one immeasurably great man who was strong enough to think of himself as the spiritual ruler of mankind and to bend history to his purpose, is hanging upon it still. That is his victory and his reign.[7]

Mental illness was no longer a question. Schweitzer had lifted Jesus from the psychiatric couch by justifying his unusual behavior in the context of an all-consuming eschatological purpose. The man from Nazareth was ruled sane, but his deity and maturity remained open for debate.

A Scholarly Divorce

After Schweitzer, psychology and theology parted company. Psychology became more mechanistic as it gained academic stature. Theologians left the field to battle social concerns. By World War II, Sigmund Freud's "psychoanalysis," John Watson's "behaviorism," and Skinner's "operant conditioning" dominated psychological interests. None of these theories of personality made room for the spirit or soul of man. In reaction, Christians either attacked psychology or uncritically accepted its conclusions. Shortly after the war, I took my first course in psychology at a Christian college. Unwittingly, the instructor simply repeated the notes of his university professor. Later on, as I took advanced courses in the field, I realized that the course had been taught from a radically behavioristic, or Watsonian, point of view. Neither the instructor nor his students saw the conflict between the prayer that opened the class session and the teaching that followed.

Psychology and religion made new overtures to each other after World War II when counseling became popular. As a young seminarian in the early 1950s, I became enthralled with the prospects of making counseling psychology a part of my ministerial education, and I enrolled in a hospital program for clinical pastoral training. Without an understanding of the philosophical assumptions underlying personality theory, I became a victim of "nondirective" counseling. Carl Rogers was the psychological folk-hero of the time. He had developed a method in which the counselor reflects the feelings of the counselee, without giving direction. Theoretically, it was assumed that persons have in themselves resources for their own healing; so each day twenty-four seminarians were turned loose on patients at the university hospital as their "client-centered" chaplains. Obedient to the grading system, we were silent when we wanted to talk, nodded uh-huh as we choked down our own ideas, and parroted the patient's words by beginning each response with "You feel . . ."

One day an Episcopalian student questioned whether you can keep saying uh-huh to a dying patient. "Isn't there a time to pray, read Scripture, and introduce Jesus Christ?" he asked. My passive mood was snapped, and I realized I had been a soft touch for a humanistic theory of personality. As a discipline, Rogers's technique was excellent, but as a method tending toward cure-all claims, it violated my faith. Therefore, I joined the Episcopalian rebels as we challenged our instructors and struggled with the problems of integrating a counseling technique with our Christian beliefs.

Shortly after my experience with clinical pastoral counseling, a graduate professor of psychology told our class that Jesus was a psychologist and counselor without peer but that no one had seriously studied him from that point of view. I realized what was wrong. Conservative scholars had avoided a study of the personality of Jesus for fear of detracting from his deity. Liberal theologians and psychologists had attacked the personality of Jesus but retreated under the incisive scholarship of Schweitzer. Thus a vacuum was left between religion and psychology that was now being filled by an on-rush of developing psychological theories. Rather than starting with the Scriptures, the new theories were the Procrustean bed, and Christianity was being cut to fit.

To counteract this trend, I began a biblical study of the personality and psychology of Jesus. Certain assumptions guided the search. First, I accepted the Scriptures as inspired by God with accuracy, authority, and relevance for the psychological needs of modern men and women. Second, rather than starting from psychological theories, I examined the particulars of Scripture and drew generalizations according to the principles of inductive Bible study. Third, modesty was to guide my observations because of the fragmentary account of the life of Jesus and the ever-present dangers of imposing psychological theory on the Scriptures or claiming more than they reveal. By listening to the Scriptures rather than dictating to them, a biblical perspective of the personality and psychology of Jesus was my goal.

Later, I was attracted to a new frontier in psychology called "psychohistory." Freud introduced the technique with his classic, but controversial, study *Moses and Monotheism*. Utilizing psychoanalytical theory and Old Testament history, Freud diagnosed Moses as having an Oedipal conflict with his father. His guilt was repressed until it exploded in violence when Moses killed the Egyptian soldier. The release of his aggression became the basis for a pattern of leadership which shaped the personality and destiny of the Israelite nation. Confidently, Freud concluded, "One man, the man Moses . . . created the Jews." [8]

Just before he died, Freud signed the autographs for another psychohistorical volume which he co-authored with William C. Bullitt. Woodrow Wilson was the subject of the study. Rather than reaching back into the prehistorical Oedipal conflict as he had done with Moses, Freud judged that Woodrow Wilson was an emotionally sick man who had an acute need to fail, which probably arose from his guilt over an uncertain masculinity. Wilson's pathological problem was then projected onto the world scene when he proposed his Fourteen Points for the League of Nations—an idealistic venture that was doomed to fail. As usual, Freud read history as an extension of personality, not as an interacting force.

Psychohistory gained credibility with the work of Erik Erikson, a psychoanalyst who studied both Martin Luther and Mahatma Gandhi. As did Freud, Erikson analyzed the personality of his famous subject and projected it onto the screen of history by what he called "The Event." In Luther's case, there was the hint of an Oedipal conflict when the young priest rebelled against the pope as a father-figure, but "The Event" in Luther's life was the moment of rage when he heard Johann Tetzel, the seller of indulgences, singing outside his window:

> When your coin into the coffer rings,
> The soul of your loved one
> From purgatory springs. [9]

Erikson's book *Gandhi's Truth* [10] is equally intriguing. Gandhi was relatively unknown until "The Event" when he reluctantly recommended a strike against the mill owners because of working conditions. In reaction against aggression, Gandhi chose a hunger fast to demonstrate nonviolent protest. The die was cast for a nation to be molded by the profile of a personality.

Freud and Erikson differed in their views of psychohistory. Cultural and historical factors were almost totally ignored by Freud. To him, history was just "personality writ large." Erikson, by contrast, respected the give-and-take of personality and culture in shaping historical events. Despite this disagreement, they stood together on Freud's conclusion that "a great man influences his contemporaries in two ways— through his personality and through the ideas for which he stands." [11] Without espousing Freudian theory, I asked myself whether the technique might help me answer the question, How did the personality of Jesus influence his ideas, his work, and his impact on human history? A psychohistory of Jesus became a part of my quickening interest.

A SHAKY MARRIAGE

Psychology and Christianity have often flirted, sometimes curtsied, and occasionally danced. Confusion still reigns. At one extreme are the philosopher-psychologists who have advanced their theories as panaceas and utopias. For example, B. F. Skinner's *Walden Two* elevates "operant conditioning" to a faith with an evangelistic outreach. Some research psychologists are not far behind. While admitting that the state of the science is still in infancy, they contend that ultimately psychology could lead to the prediction and control of all human behavior.

Psychiatrists and counseling psychologists have moved closer to religion than have their experimental colleagues.

A revival of the writings of Carl Jung has grown out of his holistic and mystical interest in persons. Victor Frankl, Rollo May, and Paul Tournier are other noted psychiatrists who have searched for reconciliation between psychology and religion.

Christians have been swept along with the popular tide of counseling psychology. Some scholars in colleges and seminaries are serious students of the field and grapple with the conflicts and consistencies between Christianity and psychology. Others have rushed like lemmings to the sea to train for counseling practice. In seminaries, pastoral psychology is often the most popular curriculum. Institutes that offer graduate study in the field have long waiting lists. At the undergraduate level, new offerings in Christian ministries reflect the emphasis on counseling in the church and related agencies. As might be expected in this opportunistic climate, some authors, consultants, and practitioners limit the need for psychological knowledge to a few biblical propositions that are organized into a counseling theory and put into practice.

A ready market for popular psychology with a religious touch exists among Christians as well as with the general public. Pastors and laymen flock to attend "communication" seminars where the participants are urged to drop their masks and become real persons. Ironically, the Christian community has praised sessions in "exposure therapy" while condemning "sensitivity training" as manipulative brainwashing.

Publishers find that books on Christian social responsibility gather dust on the shelves, but writings by Christian authors who can combine their spiritual experience with psychological introspection are repeatedly reprinted. Keith Miller's *A Taste of New Wine* and *The Second Touch* are in this category. Daring to confess his humanity, Miller struck a responsive chord in every Christian who has felt the pressure to play perfect when he or she has only been forgiven.

Christians also have crowded out seminars and workshops that combine biblical and psychological principles for understanding personal motivation and human relationships. Several years ago, I introduced an unknown young man to a group of 175 people who had signed up for a new seminar in parent-child relationships. Utilizing a mixture of biblical propositions, elementary psychology, and common sense, the seminar has mushroomed into a national phenomenon that thousands attend time and again. Thousands more tune in weekly to hear a television preacher mix biblical premises and psychological affirmations in a renamed version of Norman Vincent Peale's "Power of Positive Thinking." Spectacular success in such ventures confirms the need of people for guidelines by which they can understand themselves and their problems.

JESUS: POINT OF INTEGRATION

Sound scholarship and critical analysis are needed to sort out these efforts to combine religion and psychology. Otherwise, the two fields are enemies without cause or bedfellows without communion. For a Christian, the power of *discrimination* originates through the Holy Spirit who reveals Jesus Christ. Sub-Christian or super-Christian theories and practices, whether in psychology or religion, do injustice to the nature of the person who was fully God and fully man. Therefore, in weighing the relative merits of movements that are trying to reconcile Christianity and psychology, the discriminating question must be, Is the divine-human nature of Jesus the central focus for both theory and practice?

Integration between Christianity and psychology is as important as the power of discrimination. By definition, psychology and religion will always be in tension. Forced efforts to bring them together around a common idea or a compatible method are temporary, at best. A third point is needed outside the tension line: a synthesis that each advocate recognizes as objective and superior.

Without apology, my thesis is that Jesus Christ is the point of *synthesis*. Accordingly, in response to The Question, Who is Jesus? (part 1) our study proceeds to these integrative answers: Jesus is a *real and complete human being who developed maturity through discipline* (part 2, The Personality of Jesus). From Jesus' own experience he became a *perceptive student of human behavior who taught the principles of personhood and the dynamics of wholeness* (part 3, The Psychology of Jesus). Then, as a *counselor, teacher, and minister,* he demonstrated his maturity and understanding to bring healing in his relationships with people (part 4, The Practice of Jesus).

Who is Jesus? If he is a mature human being, a knowledgeable student of human behavior, and an effective worker in human relationships, he is *Jesus, Our Model* (part 5, The Answer).

A risky venture awaits us. When C. S. Lewis was being pursued by God, he wrote, "A young man who wishes to remain a sound Atheist cannot be too careful of his reading . . . God is . . . very unscrupulous." [12] If we wish to remain the same, we cannot be too careful to avoid a collision course with the Word of God, but if we dare to share the hope that "we shall be like him" (1 John 3:2, KJV), we can never know enough about the God-man Jesus. At least we can edge up to the mystery and perhaps, in the process, change our lives.

Part Two

THE PERSONALITY OF JESUS

"The word of God became a human being and lived among us . . . "
John 1:14

Chapter Two

HIS HUMANITY

JESUS WAS fully human. To us, humanity means frailty and failure; hence, our dilemma. We need a God who is beyond us and yet one with whom we can identify. That was God's intention in the Incarnation. "The word of God became a human being and lived among us" (John 1:14). In Jesus, God put himself into a real man who might have lived next door.

A THEOLOGY OF JESUS' MANHOOD

Scripture affirms the humanity of Jesus as a cardinal truth. When John was inspired to write "the word of God became a human being," he was closing the gap between the God who is "wholly other" and the God who "lived among us."

A visionary in mind and a romantic in heart, John would

have preferred to write about the God of eternal love and mystery. But as an inspired instrument, he saw the reality of the Word and the light becoming bone, flesh, and muscle. Later, God honored John's visionary mind with the Revelation of things to come and also balanced his romantic heart with the privilege of writing an Epistle based on the empirical evidence of a God he had seen, heard, and touched. John's witness of the humanity of Jesus is credible by contradiction. Only *truth* breaking through to a mystic and *fact* arresting a romantic could bring him to announce that "the word of God became a human being and lived among us."

Paul, perhaps more status-conscious that John, put the Incarnation into the perspective of the role that Jesus assumed as a human being:

> For he, who had always been God by nature, did not cling to his prerogatives as God's equal, but stripped himself of all privilege by consenting to be a slave by nature and being born as mortal man. And, having become man, he humbled himself by living a life of utter obedience, even to the extent of dying, *and the death he died was the death of a common criminal"* (Phil. 2:6–8, italics mine).

Two gigantic downward steps are implied in Paul's *kenotic* (emptying) revelation. Jesus divested himself of his divine privileges to become a man, but then, by "utter obedience," he took on the consequences of a criminal, the lowliest of men.

Sociologists suggest that each of us needs someone to "look down on." The upper class gets status by looking down on the middle class; the middle class, on the lower class; and the lower class, on an ethnic minority. Such a theory helps explain class discrimination and frustration at the bottom of the social totem pole where there is no one else upon whom to look down. "Wops," "kikes," "Newfies," "niggers," "Polacks," and "coonasses" are the derogatory tags put on people at the bottom.

Jesus emptied himself of more than the glory of his position with the Father. Entering the human status system at the lower level as a Nazarene carpenter, he was pressed down to the bottom rung where all human dignity was lost in a criminal's death on the cross. In that shameful social condition, Jesus had no one to "look down on," but from that position he became fully man for every person and every class.

While biblical authors never doubted that Jesus was fully man and fully God, heretics in the early church soon raised the question. The Docetae doubted the reality of Jesus' human body. They contended that physical functions, such as eating and sleeping, were illusions to those who observed Jesus' life. As an opening for the christological controversy, the Docetae could not reconcile the idea of God in the flesh. John answered their arguments in his first Epistle: "We are writing to you about something which has always existed yet which we ourselves actually saw and heard: something which we had opportunity to observe closely and even to hold in our hands, and yet, as we know now, was something of the very Word of life himself!" (1 John 1:1).

The apostle's case rests upon the proofs of a firsthand testimony, sensory experience, and a logical conclusion. When John the mystic used reason to build his case and John the romantic used reality to confirm it, the Docetae were hard pressed to rebut him.

Another heresy was perpetrated by the Apollinarians who disputed the fullness of Jesus' humanity. To them, he was a real man but not a complete man. They refused to believe that Jesus experienced the full range of human drives, emotions, and temptations. He might have risen to the height of human potential, but he could not have plummeted to the depths of human failure. The Epistle to the Hebrews was written to refute this position. With some of the most "humanized" words of Scripture, the author stated:

> Since, then, "the children" have a common physical nature as human beings, he also became a human being, so that by going through death as a man he might destroy him who had the power of death, that is, the devil; and might also set free those who lived their whole lives a prey to the fear of death. It is plain that for this purpose he did not become an angel; he became a *man*, in actual fact a descendant of Abraham. It was imperative that he should be made like his brothers in every respect, if he were to become a High Priest both compassionate and faithful in the things of God, and at the same time able to make atonement for the sins of the people. For by virtue of his own suffering under temptation he is able to help those who are exposed to temptation (Heb. 2:14–18).

No dimension of humanity is missing. Jesus was like us in every respect—physically driven, psychologically motivated, and spiritually tempted. In him, we see ourselves.

A God with whom we can identify is not enough. If there is to be atonement for our sins, our High Priest must be "faithful" as well as "compassionate." Adam was a human being who fell. Jesus, the second Adam, was a human being who had to be "faithful" if he were to be our Redeemer. In his Letter to the Romans, the Apostle Paul established the principle:

> We see, then, that as one act of sin exposed the whole race of men to God's judgment and condemnation, so one act of perfect righteousness presents all men freely acquitted in the sight of God. One man's disobedience placed all men under the threat of condemnation, but one man's obedience has the power to present all men righteous before God (Rom. 5:18–19).

Obedience then joins *compassion* in the case for the manhood of Jesus. Together they show why his full humanity was not a convenience or an accident but a theological necessity. Through the compassion of a real and complete man, God shows himself to us, and we understand him. Through the obedience of a real and complete man, God redeems his fallen creation, and we have not only a Savior but a Master and a Model.

In sum, a biblical theology of Jesus' manhood rests upon these facts. First, eternal God became a mortal man in Jesus. Second, Jesus gave up his divine privileges in order to accept the nature of a man, the status of a slave, and the death of a criminal. Third, the reality of Jesus' humanity was tested by the sense experiences of the disciples. Fourth, the completeness of Jesus' humanity was proven by his physical needs, his psychological fears, and his spiritual temptation. Fifth, the hope for our humanity rests upon Jesus' being a compassionate man who can understand us; the hope for our salvation depends upon Jesus as an obedient man who can redeem us. Within this framework, a description of the human nature of Jesus takes on new meaning.

THE HUMAN DEVELOPMENT OF JESUS

Jesus' divine-human nature is a physical as well as a theological fact. Luke, the physician, set up the paradox when he announced that Jesus was conceived by the Holy Ghost in the womb of Mary without human agency (see Luke 1:35). The genetic puzzle has never been unraveled. Did God select certain qualities in genetic structure, chromosome mix, and the DNA code? If so, what are the personality features of the Word made flesh? Some might contend that the case for the humanity of Jesus is already refuted. Others have chosen to deny the virgin birth in order to make Jesus fully human. Logically, the genetic mystery is no greater than the Incarnation itself. Like geneticists who have not unlocked the secret of conception, we must rely upon information about Jesus' birth and development to find out if he was fully human.

Following conception, Jesus was subject to all the laws of natural human development. Luke stated as a matter of fact that Mary's baby was carried full-term and naturally born. Later, the child was circumcised, given a human name, and purified according to the requirements of the Law.

Jesus' human lineage further confirms his relationship with the family of man. In Matthew, the ancestry of Jesus is traced through the *royal* line of Abraham and David (see Matt. 1:1–17). Luke's genealogy places Jesus in the *servant* line of David and Abraham (see Luke 3:24–38). Jews, who were meticulous adherents to the purity of blood lines, never doubted Jesus' human ancestry.

After certifying Jesus' birth, infancy, and lineage, the Gospels lapse into silence about his childhood and early adulthood. Significantly, an episode from his adolescence is reported. At the age of twelve, Jesus accompanied his parents to Jerusalem for Passover and stayed behind to visit the Temple when the caravan pulled out. A miracle is often read into the Temple experience of Jesus, but contextually it is more consistent to put the event in the line of his natural development. Nothing should be taken away from Jesus' awakening intellect and God-consciousness, but neither can it be forgotten that he astonished the Temple sages by the questions he asked as well as by the answers he gave. As parents know so well, curious children can ask questions that would confound philosophers. At the age of five, my son pondered aloud, "If God the Father is God and Jesus the Son is God, how can Jesus be his own Father?" Twenty years later, our eight-year-old tag-along son asked his mother, "If you didn't have me like you didn't have my little brother, where would I be now?" I prefer to read the Temple seminar as the dawning of an intellectual and spiritual curiosity in a twelve-year-old boy who was well schooled in Jewish re-

ligion and well mothered in his special destiny. Certainly
his messianic future was in his bones.

Jesus' encounter with the scholars in the Temple was
matched by the confrontation with his parents after they
found him. If his intellect was fired in the Temple, his
independence flared when he stood before his parents.
Typically, Mary and Joseph's exhausted patience created a
crisis. If the face-off ran true to form, father reached for a
whip, but mother intervened with a plea, "Why have you
treated us like this, my son? Your father and I have been very
worried. We've looked for you everywhere!"

Parents of teenagers would not be surprised by the retort
that smacks of impudence, "But why were you looking for
me? Did you not know that I must be in my Father's house?"
(Luke 2:48–49). Injured innocence is a proven ploy in the
strategy of teenagers who are bringing up their parents.
Spiritualizers who restrict the interpretation of Jesus' response to his messianic foresight have broken the line of his
natural development. Mary and Joseph may not have
comprehended the prophetic import of their Son's reaction,
but surely they sensed the first flashes of independence that
characterized the human drive for self-identity.

Following the Temple event, Jesus went home and lived
as an obedient son through the "hidden" years of his life. A
single sentence describing those years contains two facts
about the young man. First, there was natural progression in
human development as "Jesus continued to grow." Second,
there was full human range to his development. As "Jesus
continued to grow in body and mind, he grew also in the love
of God and of those who knew him" (Luke 2:52).

We can infer other hints about the early life of Jesus from
the account of his homecoming to Nazareth. When he taught
in the synagogue, the townsfolk were astonished: "He's only
the carpenter, Mary's son, the brother of James, Joses, Judas
and Simon; and his sisters are living here with us!" (Mark

36

6:3). During the "hidden" years, Jesus had learned the carpenter's trade as the first son of a large family. Some scholars have noticed the absence of Joseph's name from the list and have concluded that Mary was a widow. If so, Jesus was also the major wage earner in the family before he embarked on his public ministry. A large family, astonished townsfolk, and a carpenter's trade all lend credence to Jesus' natural development as a complete human being.

THE HUMAN DRIVES OF JESUS

Air, water, food, sleep, and sex are potent human needs that influence personality development. The Gospels report that Jesus was subject to all these needs. His temptation began with hunger (see Luke 4:2). He used his thirst as a reason to speak to the Samaritan woman at the well (see John 4:7–8). Matthew said that "Jesus was sleeping soundly" (Matt. 8:25) when his frightened disciples awakened him during the storm at sea.

Several other physiological responses are noted in the Scriptures. Jesus wept over Jerusalem (see Luke 19:41) and Lazarus (see John 11:35). In a sideline comment John noted that "it was wintertime and Jesus was walking about inside the Temple in Solomon's cloisters" (John 10:22–23). Perhaps slapping his arms and stomping his feet, Jesus was pacing the corridor to keep warm.

Death is the most forceful witness to the physical responses of Jesus. On the cross he cried, "I am thirsty" (John 19:28), in a helpless response to body dehydration due to the loss of blood. Even more dramatically, his last "great cry" at the moment of death signaled the pain of crucifixion as a "scorpion with a thousand teeth."

The place of sex in Jesus' life remains a mystery to us. He had to have a fully developed sex drive because he was human and because "he himself has shared fully in all our experience of temptation" (Heb. 4:15). How else could he have set the standard that "every man who looks at a woman lustfully has already committed adultery with her—in his heart" (Matt. 5:28)? After all, women were a part of Jesus' life. Mary the mystic, Martha the homemaker, and Mary Magdalene the forgiven whore were his friends, but there is no intimation of a personal love affair with any of them.

The Scriptures never dodge or downplay sex. Right or wrong, saint or sinner, sexual encounters are bluntly reported. In fact, one test of biblical reliability is the frankness with which immorality is treated. Without further evidence, we can only assume that Jesus' sex drive was fully developed and expressed in a way consistent with his life and record.

Once, after a debate with the Pharisees over divorce, Jesus' disciples concluded that it was better not to marry. Jesus' reply was that marriage required a special gift that was not given everyone. Some, he said, are incapable of marriage because of birth or human action; others "have made themselves so for the sake of the kingdom of Heaven" (Matt. 19:12).

Why not accept sex as one of the human needs that Jesus subordinated to the higher purpose of the kingdom of God? He made similar decisions about water, food, and sleep at one time or another during his ministry, and ultimately he had to decide to put aside physical life itself for the fulfillment of his mission. In any case, flights of imagination about Jesus' having a marriage or affairs will have to remain in the fantasies of modern novels, but how quickly fantasy gives way to blasphemy when the imagination is evil. Having driven his patrons to boredom at the limits of perverted love, a Danish pornographer is now stumping the world seeking permission to produce a hard-core film on the sex life of Jesus.

THE FOURTH MYSTERY

Despite centuries of scholarly search, Jesus remains a mystery man. Our curiosity is whetted by the riddles of his

38

nature, and our intellect is frustrated by guesswork solutions for which we have no proof.

Three mysteries in the human development of Jesus have already unfolded before us—his genetic nature, his hidden years, and his sex life. Now, the fourth mystery looms large at the end of Jesus' life. John concluded his Gospel with an expansive, almost exorbitant claim: "Of course, there are many other things which Jesus did, and I suppose that if each one were written down in detail, there would not be room in the whole world for all the books that would have to be written" (John 21:25).

Knowing John, we might say that his mystical impulses got out of hand. But Luke, by reputation a more objective observer, reinforces John's sweeping claim by putting the last forty days of Jesus' life into a single verse:

> Before he ascended he gave his instructions, through the Holy Spirit, to the special messengers of his choice. For after his suffering he showed himself alive to them in many convincing ways, and appeared to them repeatedly over a period of forty days talking with them about the affairs of the kingdom of God (Acts 1:2-3).

Our fourth mystery is the ministry of Jesus after the Resurrection. Events are recorded from the beginning and the end of the period, but the middle is a conundrum. His appearances immediately after the Resurrection are selected examples of the "infallible proofs" (Acts 1:3, KJV) that he was alive. The Gospel record then skips to the pre-Ascension utterances of the Great Commission and the promise of the Holy Spirit. What did Jesus say and do during the forty-day interval? The silence of the record evokes other questions that are clues to the mystery.

Were Jesus' acts limited to the "infallible proofs" of his Resurrection? According to Luke, Jesus appeared and acted many times, but no act is recorded that is not a Resurrection proof. Enough is written, however, to leave no doubt that the apostles were personally convinced that Jesus was alive. They also believed that no more proof was needed other than that which was written to transmit the Resurrection as a historical fact to future generations.

Did Jesus introduce new truth when he talked with his disciples? A silent record leads us to assume that no new revelation was necessary. Rather, Jesus reinforced, expanded, and applied the principles of his earlier teaching. Only John's dialogue between Jesus and Peter tells us about the teaching-learning process of the forty-day period (see John 21:15–22). Showing compassion for a guilty man who had denied him, Jesus turned a negative encounter into a vote of confidence. If John's story is a clue, Jesus used the forty days for a leadership seminar in which he completed the learning cycle with individual attention to each apostle.

Is it possible that the resurrected nature of Jesus limited the work he could do in the last forty days? From his birth until his death, Jesus' full humanity and deity seemed to open like a morning flower before a sunrise. Death, then, was the final proof of his humanity and the ultimate experience with which we can identify in our current state. Even though Jesus still had human characteristics after the Resurrection, his nature had a qualitative difference which separated him historically and spiritually from all other individuals. Thus, when he spoke or acted after the Resurrection, his frame of reference and his public posture were changed. If the Resurrected Jesus had mounted a public platform, his choice would have been either to participate in a political coup or request a speed-up for the rapture. As a Model, he was limited to those "in the faith."

Our thoughts about the "post-Resurrection mystery" then are consistent with the developmental nature of the humanity and deity of Jesus. For a Christian, confidence is reaffirmed in the finality of the revelation of truth in the person of

Jesus during his human ministry. I compare his public silence during the post-Resurrection period with my own thoughts after giving an address or making a decision. In the middle of the night I awaken, remembering a thousand things I should have said. In Jesus' case, no postscript was needed for his ministry. The final authority of his words and the effective Model of his life are justified by the silence of his last forty days on earth. As with the other mysteries, enough is known about Jesus' post-Resurrection appearances to confirm rather than confuse our faith.

JESUS: A HUMAN BEING

Two facts are before us. By theological necessity and physical description, Jesus had to be fully human. Ancient heresies that reduced his humanity and inflated his divinity have been refuted by revelation and reason. Modern critics have fared no better. To strip Jesus of his deity makes him a liar, not a brother. The biblical alternative is to accept the essential truth that Jesus, the Son of God, was a real, complete human being. No other choice can demonstrate the full range of God's compassion for our condition or the potential for our redemption. If Jesus is not fully human, Christian theology is canceled at the center of the argument.

As a man in society, Jesus developed naturally. True, there are knowledge gaps about his nature. A genetic mystery surrounds his conception; hidden years veil young adulthood; his sex drive is known only by inference; and most of his post-Resurrection words were spoken in "executive session" with his disciples. Little is known about the "awakening" of his divine nature. Did he know he was God from birth? Was he speaking as the Son of God in the Temple at age twelve? If so, he chose to keep his identity hidden in his heart as a compact with his mother, Mary. If not, God chose to let his divine nature develop along with his human nature.

A Hebrew home, a carpenter shop, and a nondescript village made up the staging area for both revelations. How else can we identify with the God who was born a human being and lived among us?

Whatever the gaps of theology and history in the life of Jesus, God's purpose is no mystery. He gave us a *compassionate* man who *understands* us and an *obedient* man who *redeems* us. Only the incarnate Christ can explain the response of my friend who was grieving the loss of his daughter in a flash flood along the Thompson River in Colorado. When I met him two weeks after the tragedy, his eyes were sunk in dark sockets from weeping. Awkwardly, I asked, "How is it going?"

Never given to public testimony or eloquent statements, his sad eyes looked back, and he spoke almost from a trance, "The hurt goes deep, but his love goes deeper."

Without having heard the christological question, "but who do you say that I am?" my friend had given the answer.

Chapter Three

HIS TRAITS

MARK'S GOSPEL vibrates with the action of a fast-moving drama. Wasting no time on historical overtures, Mark plunges into a script that flows through active verbs and changes scenes with a color commentary of descriptive adverbs and adjectives. On a well-timed cue, he brings Jesus to center stage. Quickly entangling him in human situations, Mark builds his plot around the personality of his tragic hero. Movement for the Gospel is speeded by the commanding presence of Jesus, who acted "immediately" and "straightway" from the beginning to the end of his ministry. And in each of his encounters with life—death, sin, and suffering—another facet of the personality of Jesus is revealed. Like a dramatist who has the genius for creating characters in depth, Mark probes the motives, needs, emotions, and traits

42

of the Son of Man; yet he never loses his grasp on Jesus' total personality. When his Gospel story is told, the analysis of the human traits of the Son of Man has been synthesized with the divine character of the Son of God. To come to the same understanding, we must ask, What are the human traits of the personality of Jesus?

A Personality Profile

A personality trait is the generalized way in which an individual responds to different situations. Many psychological scales have been devised to study traits. Most of them compare two characteristics along the same dimension. For example, some common traits studied by R. B. Cattell [1] can be compared on the following scale:

Personality Dimension	Comparative Traits	
Character	Honest	Dishonest
Relationships	Gregarious	Retiring
Temperament	Forceful	Sensitive
Intelligence	Logical	Intuitive
Tolerance	Patient	Impatient
Mood	Humorous	Serious

On this scale, a profile might show a person tending to be honest, retiring, sensitive, logical, impatient, and humorous; or it would not be surprising to see the personality contour of a person who is dishonest, gregarious, forceful, intuitive, patient, and serious. Such variations are based on three assumptions: (1) traits are not fixed but vary from time to time and from situation to situation, that is, a person may be honest in one setting and dishonest in another; (2) traits are not interdependent, that is, a logical person need not be patient; and (3) traits are not grouped in either-or categories, that is, a person is neither totally gregarious nor totally retiring.

A further assumption is that there is enough consistency in human behavior to build a personality profile of unique, dominant, and complementary traits. *Unique* traits set persons apart as individuals. For example, every social group has a jester whose name would be uniquely identified with a humorous trait. Clusters of traits tend to show the *dominant* characteristics of a person. Whether the expectation is valid or not, a poet is assumed to be retiring, sensitive, intuitive, and serious. When a trait is an exception to the cluster, it is designated *complementary*. For instance, if a poet breaks out of a pattern of intuitive intelligence with the surprise of a tightly reasoned argument, the logical trait is complementary to his or her intuition. Personalities have a code of consistency. What appear to be opposite traits are always members of the supporting cast in the total drama of personality.

Complex personalities, such as Jesus, have more than their share of unique and complementary traits. Rich variations spin off from a small cluster of dominant characteristics. In every encounter, new dimensions of personality are revealed, and surprise responses make the experience unforgettable. At best, a profile of the personality of Jesus is just the starting point for the unexpected.

THE CHARACTER OF JESUS

One unique trait set Jesus apart from all other personalities. On the scale from honest to dishonest, his integrity was unblemished. Unequivocally, Peter declared, "He was guilty of no sin nor the slightest prevarication" (1 Pet. 2:22). Earlier, Jesus himself had already thrown out the unanswered challenge, "Which of you can prove me guilty of sin?"

(John 8:46). Even after Pilate's biased cross-examination, the governor had to admit, "I find nothing criminal about him at all" (John 18:39).

No other human being ever stood such scrutiny. As ancient merchants held pottery up to the light of the sun to detect the telltale scar of wax that filled in the cracks of faulty vessels, Jesus' character was exposed to friends and enemies. When all the evidence was in, he was pronounced "sincere" or "without wax," a commendation reserved for only a flawless creation.

Does Jesus' total integrity reduce his humanity? Or another way to ask the question is, Did Jesus have to sin to be fully human? From either an empirical or a theological viewpoint, the answer is no. Jesus had all the physical, psychological, and social needs of a man. He developed naturally and participated in the full range of human experience. Most of all, he had the freedom of choice. Conscious decisions until the day he died kept him free from sin. Therefore, to argue that Jesus had to sin to be human is to confuse an empirical description with a theological issue. Jesus had all the characteristics of a human being—needs, development, experience, and choice. The fact that all other persons have sinned does not rule out a man of unique integrity by choice. Otherwise, there is no freedom. Theology aside, Jesus' unique trait of total integrity had to be a human possibility.

Without full humanity and total integrity, the doctrine of salvation cannot be established. As a man, Jesus experienced every aspect of human temptation. Like us, he felt the pervasive power of evil—both internally and externally. But unlike us, he learned about the consequences of sin by circumstance rather than by choice. Upon his integrity was laid our iniquity in the form of guilt, alienation, suffering, and death. But for those of us who have sinned, his integrity is in our favor. Jesus' blameless life balances against sin on the scales of justice, demonstrates the meaning of love in the redemptive act, and exemplifies the freedom from sin which is possible for one who obeys God.

Of course, the paradox of a man who *could* sin and a God who *could not* is still with us. Without pretending to resolve it, we can only say that the unique trait of total integrity in the personality of Jesus is humanly possible and theologically essential.

THE RELATIONSHIPS OF JESUS

When Jesus had a choice, he preferred to be alone or in the company of a small band of disciples or friends. Mark recorded twelve different occasions when Jesus chose solitude over people or close friends over the crowd. Sometimes it was for prayer and meditation; at other times it was for teaching and relaxation. On seven other occasions, Jesus avoided public attention by commanding people he had healed to "tell no man." Even the triumphal entry seems to have a reluctant hero. A subdued tone of resolution rather than exuberance qualified Jesus' response to public acclaim.

Occasionally, Jesus sought a social setting. He enjoyed himself at the marriage in Cana (see John 2:1–11). In contrast to the asceticism of John the Baptist, Jesus' enemies called him "a drunkard and a glutton" (Matt. 11:19). Certainly, more than one party would be necessary to uphold the accusation. Gospel writers, however, gave more attention to Jesus' close relationships with a limited number of people. He called his disciples "friends" (John 15:14). Even though Jesus said he had no place to lay his head, the homes of friends—Peter, Matthew, Zaccheus, Simon the leper, Martha, Mary, and Lazarus—were places where he stayed.

Perhaps Jesus found himself cast in the role of a celebrity

who prefers privacy but has a public responsibility. Recently, I was asked to introduce a famous "voice" at a banquet. As I approached the personage in the anteroom before the meeting, my ears were tuned for that magical sound. Instead I was greeted by a passive voice, soft if not reticent. During the dinner, we chatted casually about children, hobbies, and mutual friends. My introduction was the "hot button." Our guest sprang to his feet, challenged the microphone, turned on his broadcasting voice, and ricocheted a smattering of news notes over his transfixed audience for fifty minutes. After applause and autographs, he fled the scene for the privacy of a hotel room. At first I tagged him just another performer who was anointed by public acclaim, but his courage in stating his convictions dispelled that notion. I could only conclude that he was subdued in person but spirited in performance by the grip of his message.

If I had been in Capernaum when Jesus stood in the synagogue and announced "The Spirit of the Lord is upon me, Because he anointed me to preach good tidings" (Luke 4:18), I might have come to the same conclusion about him. Naturally a retiring man, Jesus became a spell-binding, authoritative figure when he spoke the truth in the Spirit. But when given an option, he preferred to be alone on a mountain, in a boat with disciples, or at dinner with close friends. Jesus was a private person with a public responsibility.

On a comparative scale of traits, Jesus would appear to be more retiring than gregarious. Such a description fits the personality of a small-town man who worked with wood rather than with people. If so, it is no wonder that his townsfolk were astonished when they measured his eloquent preaching against their memory of a carpenter of few words. All this changed when the Spirit of the Lord anointed Jesus for public ministry. Crowds followed him wherever he went, and public exposure became his fate. Still, when given an option, he retreated to a mountain, a boat, or the home of a friend. A part of his depth was the privacy of his person.

THE TEMPERAMENT OF JESUS

Sensitivity is a dominant trait of Jesus, highlighted by the Gospel of Mark. At the beginning of Jesus' ministry, a leper came to him and said, " 'If you want to, you can make me clean.' Jesus was *filled with pity* for him, and stretched out his hand and placed it on the leper, saying, 'Of course I want to—*be clean!*' " (Mark 1:40–41, first italics mine). Mark saw the same deep feeling at work when he noted that Jesus had pity for the masses of people who were milling about "like sheep without a shepherd" (Mark 6:34). Later on, in a similar situation, he heard Jesus himself say that his heart went out to the hungry crowd (see Mark 8:2).

Jesus' sensitivity was not selective. As he pitied the sick and reached out to the hungry, he empathized with the dilemma of the wealthy young ruler. Jesus looked at him with love even though Jesus had to speak a truth that could cost the young man eternal life (see Mark 10:21).

A sensitive spirit is especially vulnerable to personal wounding. When Jesus prayed in the Garden, he was "horror-stricken and desperately depressed." Returning to his disciples, he told them, "My heart is nearly breaking . . . Stay here and keep watch for me" (Mark 14:33–34). Nineteenth-century critics used this scene to prove that Jesus was psychotic. Had they explored his sensitivity rather than his sanity, their answers would have been different. Jesus was absorbing the fear of death that haunts every man. The sensitivity that had made him so responsive to the needs of others was now turned inward as soul-rending grief in his final struggle.

Timidity should not be confused with sensitivity. Jesus

could be as forceful as the situation demanded. When he preached, his words had the "ring of authority" (Mark 1:22). A magnetic boldness put compulsion in his call to Andrew and Peter just when they were casting their nets (see Mark 1:17). Mark was impressed when Jesus "cut him short and spoke sharply" (Mark 1:24–25) to an evil spirit that began to mock Jesus' name and make fun of his deeds. Also, there was no hesitation when Jesus put the jeering crowd out of the house so that he could heal Jairus's daughter (see Mark 5:40–41). Forcefulness and sensitivity were complementary traits in the personality of Jesus, for he was assertive when speaking the truth and warm when working with persons.

THE INTELLIGENCE OF JESUS

Intellectual traits are compared on a continuum from close-ordered logic to mystical intuition. Usually we think of Jesus as a person of intuitive intelligence. John, for example, attributed unusual perceptive powers to Jesus when he wrote, "He did not need anyone to tell him what people were like: he understood human nature" (John 2:25). A common error is to assume that this insight was more divine than human, but we must not forget that native intelligence, personalized sensitivity, and perceptive observation are human components of the same gift. Mark saw practical intuition at work when the scribes accused Jesus of blasphemy and Jesus "realized instantly what they were thinking" (Mark 2:8). Their words betrayed them. In another instance, Mark linked Jesus' intuition with his sensitivity. Criticized for healing the man with a withered hand on the sabbath day, Jesus confounded his accusers with some questions:

"Is it right to do good on the Sabbath day, or to do harm? Is it right to save life or to kill?"

There was a dead silence. Then Jesus, deeply hurt as he *sensed their inhumanity*, looked round in anger at the faces surrounding him, and said to the man,
"Stretch out your hand!" (Mark 3:4–5, italics mine).

Jesus' keen perception detected not only hypocrisy and inhumanity but human need. When the woman reached out to touch the hem of his garment, "At once Jesus *knew intuitively* that power had gone out of him" (Mark 5:30, italics mine). Before body language or the psychology of touch, Jesus was schooled in the powers of intuition.

Another indicator of Jesus' intuitive intelligence was his skill in teaching by parable. Word pictures, similes, and analogies are tools of gifted minds. Popular opinion identifies genius with complexity. To the contrary, most creative minds can simplify the truth through word pictures. Their command of a whole visual field permits them to see new solutions to old problems. Who hasn't chuckled at the thought of the truck jammed into an overpass because the driver failed to read the "Low Clearance" sign? After wreckers arrived and failed to extricate the vehicle, a boy came by, took one look at the wreck, and suggested, "Why not let some air out of the tires and drive the truck out?" His visual perception of the field provided a solution everyone else had missed. As a master of the commonplace and a teacher of the visual arts, Jesus was equally creative in communicating new truth.

The range of Jesus' intelligence was not limited to perceptual insights. He was equally at home in situations that demanded the discipline of the logical mind. Debates with the scribes and Pharisees were conducted in the tradition of precise scholarly dialogue. He could turn the logic of the Pharisees to his own advantage by the counterattack, "I am going to ask *you* a question" (Mark 11:29, italics mine), or he could confound the scribes with their own authority by verbatim quotations from the Scriptures (see Mark 12:29–

31). Even though intuition appears to have been the dominant trait of Jesus' intelligence, he had the complementary quality of a disciplined, logical mind.

THE TOLERANCE OF JESUS

Frustration tests our threshold of tolerance on a scale from patience to impatience. Minimal frustration may throw some people into rage. Others with higher thresholds can be severely thwarted without reaction. As a personality trait, patience is best measured under stress.

To illustrate the level of tolerance, a psychology teacher once told of a man who was awakened at one o'clock in the morning by a telephone call. An exuberant voice said, "Hello, is Jonesy there?"

"No," the sleeper emphatically answered. "You have the wrong number."

At 2:00 A.M. the phone rang again. Slower to awake and longer to answer, the sleeper heard again, "Hello, is Jonesy there?"

"No!" the retort came back. "I told you before you had the wrong number, and now I want to get some sleep!" He slammed down the telephone.

An hour later the 3:00 A.M. call came. Even though the first jingle was heard by the man who had been wide awake for an hour, he let it ring. With maddening persistence, the bell continued until he picked up the phone, primed to release a fusillade of profanity. From the receiver a voice chirped, "Hi, this is Jonesy. Have there been any calls for me?"

The first call produced *consternation,* the second *exasperation,* and the third *frustration*. Situational stress had moved the awakened sleeper from a confusing question to the edge of an emotional explosion and on to a baffling enigma.

By reputation, Jesus was a tolerant man. With children,

sinners, and honest doubters, his tolerance seemed to know no bounds. Time after time, he used his patience to defuse volatile situations. Disarming answers kept the scribes and Pharisees from springing their death traps. When the disciples saw him walking on the water toward them and screamed in fright, Jesus "at once *spoke quietly* to them, 'It's all right, it is I myself; don't be afraid!'" (Mark 6:49–50, italics mine).

On the other hand, episodes in which Jesus lost patience blaze a trail through the Gospel of Mark. After using a parable to teach the crowd that a person is defiled from within, not from without, the disciples asked for an explanation. Jesus answered but not before he gritted his teeth to say, "Oh, are you as dull as they are?" (Mark 7:18). In another instance, when the disciples lacked the power to heal an epileptic boy, Jesus wondered aloud, "How long must I put up with you?" A moment later, the father of the boy begged, "But if you can do anything, please take pity on us and help us." In mimicry, Jesus retorted, *"If you can do anything!* Everything is possible to the man who believes" (see Mark 9:18–23).

Tension took its toll on Jesus' patience toward the close of his ministry. Cursing the fig tree and cleansing the Temple appear out of character for Jesus. His own hunger prompted him to curse the fig tree that had leaves but no fruit in early summer (see Mark 11:14). Jesus' own zeal, according to the prophet, ate at him when he threw out the Temple money-changers he had seen so many times before (see Mark 11:15–17). In the latter days of his ministry, Jesus became caustic in debate. When Pharisees and members of Herod's party tried to trap him by splitting his loyalty between Caesar and God, Jesus shot back, "Why try this trick on me?" Staggered by the reply, the Pharisees shifted their attack from debate to conspiracy (see Mark 12:13–17).

Jesus knew what it was to explore the outer limits of human frustration; his patience was stretched by friends and foes. Unless Mark unduly mirrored his own petulance in his writing, Jesus frequently showed an impatient trait. Frustration may be part of the price for a man with a mission who gets involved with people.

THE MOOD OF JESUS

Individual moods move in many dimensions. On our scale of personality, mood is measured by the range between humorous and serious traits. Contrary to Nietzsche's indictment of Jesus as "the gray Galilean," Jesus had to have a sense of humor. How else could he have "understood what was in man" and not lost hope? We sometimes forget that genuine humor is never a belly laugh. Jesus saw comedy in the human condition because he had an acute sense of the ludicrous. Laughable, pungent barbs were created out of a camel crawling through the eye of a needle, harlots walking into the kingdom of God ahead of priests, and a piece of wood the size of a log in a man's eye.

Man, in perspective, is the greatest laugh of all, particularly when self-righteousness is at stake. Lord Thomas Macaulay once noted, "We know of no spectacle so ridiculous as the British public in one of its periodic fits of morality." Self-righteousness in an eternal perspective was the prime target for Jesus' humor.

Overall, though, Jesus was serious. From painful experience, he had learned the value behind the admonition to his disciples, "Let your 'yes' be a plain 'yes' and your 'no' be a plain 'no' " (Matt. 5:37). A man with an urgent mission, Jesus was impelled along a straight line of serious purpose; yet he had a quality that is usually found in great persons. By laughing at the pretenses of humanity, he was laughing at himself.

JESUS' PERSONALITY PROFILE

Drawing together this description of the unique, dominant, and complementary traits of Jesus, a profile of his personality emerges:

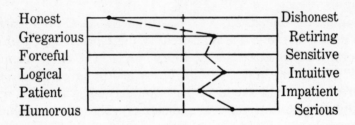

Honest		Dishonest
Gregarious		Retiring
Forceful		Sensitive
Logical		Intuitive
Patient		Impatient
Humorous		Serious

At the core of Jesus' personality is the unique trait of his *integrity*. Clustering around this distinguishing characteristic are the dominant traits of a *retiring, sensitive, intuitive, impatient, serious* person. But to cast Jesus in a stereotype is to ignore the complementary traits that sprang from the depth of his resources and the breadth of his mission. Invariably, he broke out of the mold with a gregarious hug, a forceful act, a logical argument, and a hearty laugh. Complementary traits neither neutralized nor neuroticized the personality of Jesus; rather they added richness to the quality of his person and range to the fullness of his humanity.

If the interpretation of Jesus' personality traits is advanced another step, he tended to be more introverted than extroverted. Common usage defines *introversion* as "weak and undesirable," in contrast with the strength and attraction of an extrovert. Psychology refutes such an odious comparison. Only a difference in orientation separates the types. An extrovert gets clues for behavior from *external relationships;*

an introvert is guided by his or her own *internalized values*. David Riesman, in his classic work *The Lonely Crowd*, draws a similar distinction between *other-directed* and *inner-directed* persons.[2] A rotating antenna on the head of an other-directed person constantly scans the environment for cues to guide behavior. By contrast, an inner-directed person has a built-in gyroscope which provides balance and direction from internalized values.

Even though personalities lean one way or the other, there is a bit of the extrovert and the introvert in each of us. Jesus' behavior seemed motivated by his internalized values. While he did not ignore external relationships in his behavioral responses, his primary cues came from his inner-directed sense of purpose.

Isaiah's rendering of Jesus as the "Suffering Servant" confirms the cluster of Jesus' traits and his introverted tendencies:

> In God's eyes he was like a tender green shoot, sprouting from a root in dry and sterile ground. But in our eyes there was no attractiveness at all, nothing to make us want him. We despised him and rejected him—a man of sorrows, acquainted with bitterest grief. We turned our backs on him and looked the other way when he went by. He was despised and we didn't care (Isa. 53:2-3, TLB).

JESUS: A REAL AND COMPLETE MAN

A dynamic view of Jesus' physical needs and personality traits has now come into focus. Two unique characteristics set him apart: physiologically, his response to the sex drive is inferred but unknown; psychologically, his personal integrity is unbroken. Between these distinctions is the full range of human needs, emotions, and conflicts. Through natural development, Jesus' personality was organized around a cluster of dominant personality traits. Descriptively, he was

reserved, sensitive, intuitive, impatient, and serious. An introverted person tends to exhibit similar qualities, being motivated by his or her own internal values more than by the
press of external relationships.

No offense should be taken at this view of Jesus' human
nature. His personality profile does not detract from his deity
but reinforces the truth that he was like us in every respect.
We have our own mysteries of motivation, our own packages
of peculiarities, and our own surprising responses. Jesus was
a man who had to live with his humanness as we have to live
with ours.

Artists have embraced the truth of the humanity of Jesus
better than psychologists or theologians. Human, almost tragic "Christ-figures" appear in such diverse forms as Raskolni-
kov in Dostoevski's *Crime and Punishment,* the clown in the
contemporary film *The Parable,* and Snoopy in Schulz's *Pea-
nuts.* However controversial these caricatures of Jesus may
be, they are true to Isaiah's portrait: "We turned our backs
on him and looked the other way when he went by." But
even after rejection, Christ-figures do not go away. Uncon-
sciously, if not unwillingly, we find ourselves weeping when
they lose, cheering when they win, and crying out for the
hope of their indomitable spirit.

Jesus, a real and complete *man,* produces the same reaction. At first, our sensibilities are shocked by the thought of
God in the flesh. A personality profile is an insult until we
need a God who has stood in our shoes. Then and only then
do we understand the purpose and meaning of the incarnation. If Jesus was to be a compassionate brother, it *was* im-
perative that he be a man, not an angel.

More is required of the personality of Jesus than the evidence that he is our equal. Peter claimed, "Christ . . . left
you a personal example, and wants you to follow in his steps"
(1 Pet. 2:21). With Peter's words, attention now shifts from
the characteristics of Jesus' human nature to the quality of

his personal development. He may be our *equal*, but is he our *example*? A psychologist would ask, Was Jesus a *mature* man? To answer the question, we must turn again to the Scriptures.

Chapter Four

HIS MATURITY

Every person needs a maturing model. Fifteen years ago, my first mentor in the college presidency died. After the funeral, his widow sought me out to say, "James left some things for you." Some days later, they arrived—his doctoral cap and gown, a leather-bound copy of Thomas à Kempis's *The Imitation of Christ*, and C. S. Lewis's *Surprised by Joy*.

Needless to say, Dr. James Gregory's influence on my life has continued. For more than ten years, I wore a mortar board that was too small and an academic robe that was too long. If I were to name two books other than the Bible that shaped my life, *The Imitation of Christ* and *Surprised by Joy* would lead the list. By life and legacy, Dr. Gregory continues as a "significant other" for me.

Is Jesus a maturing human model for us? We know he was a real and complete man with whom we can identify in struggle and spirit, but, like us, his humanity did not guarantee his maturity. Choices had to be made for the purpose, direction, and goal of his life. If Jesus developed the stature of a whole and effective human being, he too becomes a "significant other" who deserves a hearing and a following.

THE EVENT

Instant maturity is a fallacy. Out of a background of hereditary and environmental factors, individuals move toward their potential as persons on consistent trend lines.

Class reunions are usually filled with surprises. When old grads meet, the classic comment is, "Oh, I didn't recognize you without your acne." Two years ago, I returned to my twenty-fifth high-school reunion. A few former classmates had changed beyond immediate recognition. Consistency ruled, however, in gestures, inflections, laughs, and mannerisms. As we traced life histories of careers and families, high-school trends were projected with a frightening predictability.

Two decades of administrative work further confirm my belief in the consistency of behavioral trends. Time and again, I have hired people who had potential for success in teaching or administration but with a flaw that required change. Almost without exception, the end result was failure because the weakness persisted. For instance, a charming and creative young man was appointed to a second-line position with a view to advancement to a director's post. His recommendations sparkled except that he had trouble with management follow-through. For two years, we worked together on a personalized development program. Verbally and graphically, he presented promising professional growth plans. Some goals were accomplished but usually under pressure. Then when the directorship opened up and I appointed him to the position with the idea of "growing him" into the role, evidently the added supervisory stress reopened the weakness. Within two years, I had to let him go because of performance lags in follow-through that were aggravated by creative and well-conceived management goals. As an administrative rule-of-thumb, I now make appointments and promotions on the assumption that personal developmental trends persist and that consistent growth rather than radical change must guide my decisions.

Once the premise of consistency in human development is accepted, the uneven nature of growth can be considered. People grow and change by stops, starts, jumps, and fallbacks along a trend line. Ross Mooney, a psychologist friend, once compared human development to the exercise of walking. A body is in balance when standing still. In order to walk, however, imbalance must be risked as one foot moves forward. In that state of disequilibrium, the body has a natural drive for stability; so the trailing foot is signaled forward and balance is regained. Similarly, human development moves through states of balance, imbalance, consolidation, and balance again. Imbalance is a phase that may range from mild adjustments to traumatic changes. Seldom, however, is the predisposed direction of the person altered. Even a psychotic break is best described as a "jump" along a trend line brought on by a precipitating event.

Growth toward maturity is also uneven in speed though consistent in direction. Events and circumstances, problems and opportunities, can evoke pivotal decisions that speed up or slow down movement toward personal maturity. Frequently, those decisions are so significant that they engage every facet of human personality and leave an indelible imprint on the life and work of individuals. Psychohistory, a frontier field of psychology, writes the biographies of great persons by identifying "The Event" that shaped and altered their ideas, work, and impact on history.

Luke established the consistent trend line on which the

potential maturity of Jesus could be projected. With the keenness of a physician's diagnosis, he made this biographical note: "As Jesus continued to grow in body and mind, he grew also in the love of God and of those who knew him" (Luke 2:52). No more developmental information is given until Jesus' public debut at the time of his baptism. Here, God broke into the trend line by confirming the deity of Jesus through a settling dove and a sonorous voice: "This is my beloved Son, in whom I am well pleased" (Matt. 3:17, KJV). In effect, imbalance was created in the dual nature of Jesus. Before he could begin his ministry, Jesus had to make some pivotal decisions at the intersection where his physical drives, psychological needs, and spiritual mission converged. As a public figure who would be exposed on all fronts at once and as the new Adam upon whom the redemption of all persons rested, it was essential that Jesus be a maturing human Model as well as the confirmed Son of God.

Psychohistorians of such personalities as Moses, Luther, Wilson, and Gandhi have found turning points, called "The Event," in the lives of their subjects.[1] By their definition, "The Event" is an episode in which an individual's personality is stamped first into his or her ideas, then into his or her work, and eventually into history itself.

In Jesus' life "The Event" was his temptation. After being filled with the Holy Spirit at baptism, Jesus was led into the desert where he fasted forty days before being tempted by the devil. Thirty years of natural development had brought him to this moment. Now he had to make some decisions that would determine the impact of his personality upon his ideas and mission. The temptation was "The Event," and personal maturity was the issue at stake.

Before turning directly to the temptation, we must establish a base of understanding about the psychological needs of a human being and the criteria for personal maturity. Against this background, we can study the temptation as

62

"The Event" that projected the personality of Jesus into history.

JESUS' PSYCHOLOGICAL NEEDS

As a human being, Jesus shared our psychological as well as our physical needs. By nature, he needed *self-preservation, self-actualization,* and *self-integrity.*

Self-preservation is simply the basic "will to live." In *Here to Stay,* John Hersey tells the true stories of people who performed extraordinary feats in their struggle to survive.[2] For instance, an elderly woman led the way for the rescue of a group of people stranded in a collapsing building during a flash flood. While dangling two stories in the air, she went hand-over-hand on a rope over the rising waters. By all standards of human strength, she should have died in the flood. Only the conscious and unconscious "will to live" saved her.

Hersey also tells about John F. Kennedy. As the commander of a PT-boat, he swam for help for his crew after the boat had been shot out from under them. He tried to swim several miles across the channel between small Pacific islands only to be caught in the current. Even though he lost consciousness, he continued to drift and swim through the night until the next morning. Except for the will to live, he would have been swept out to sea and drowned.

Each of us shares the primary drive for *self-preservation.* Death has a "sting" because we want to live. Whether diseased or threatened, we fight to survive. One symbol for the despair that afflicts modern man is the suicide rate. Statistics for self-destruction seem to rise in direct proportion to the desacralization of society. As usual, the tender young are the victims of the trend as their suicide ratio jumps out of proportion to their share of the population. Whatever romance with death might have been encouraged by Alfred Alvarez's

book *The Savage God,* self-destruction symbolizes a sick society. In fact, the disease may reach beyond the obvious.
Preliminary research reports have pointed out suicidal tendencies in heart and cancer deaths. Perhaps in the mysterious
link between mind and body, the loss of self-respect can lead
to self-destruction in variant forms. Legally wrong, psychologically sick, and spiritually sinful, self-destruction cannot
be justified in any form.

When Jesus chose to die, he was neither nursing suicidal
tendencies nor capitalizing on a martyr complex. Death was
the ultimate sacrifice for him. Certainly a man who promised
others an "abundant life" had to have a fully developed desire to live.

Self-actualization is the inherent pull on a person to grow
toward his or her human potential. Ego is not wrong. To be
fully human is to develop a concept of self-worth that cannot
be demeaned. Even an infant's cry is a test of self-worth.
Whether the cry is punished or ignored, finely tuned sensors
take a reading on the baby's role and worth in the surrounding environment. Later on, a child "tests the limits" by
good and bad behavior in the continuing search for self-
actualization. An adolescent will rebel against parents in order to become an independent person. Wise parents have
learned that love, praise, and consistency are principles that
guide children through the stress of self-actualization and
build self-worth at the same time.

Jesus himself gave wide berth for ego development with
his command, "Love thy neighbor as thyself" (Mark 12:31).
In it, he laid the groundwork for a psychological theory that
contends that you cannot love others until you love yourself.
Selfishness is a form of reaction in which outward self-love
covers an inner den of self-hate.

No person can realize his or her human potential or experience redemption until the tendency to selfishness is admitted. In his torturous journey from atheism to Christianity,

C. S. Lewis came to the turning point when he unbuckled the armor he had used to protect himself against God and melted like a snowman. His heart was exposed:

> And there I found what appalled me; a zoo of lusts, a bedlam of ambitions, a nursery of fears, a harem of fondled hatreds. My name was legion.[3]

Behind the great commandment is the unspoken assumption that self-actualization begins with self-insight.

Self-integrity is a psychological need for wholeness. Physiologists employ the term *homeostasis* to describe the built-in chemical balance of the body. The same concept has been adopted by psychologists who find that people have a need for an internal psychic regulator around which the personality is organized. Otherwise, the "will to live" has no purpose, and the desire to grow has no direction.

Expressions of the need for self-integrity arise in many fields. When psychology was a discipline in swaddling clothes, theories of human personality tended to be analytical, dissecting mind and motivation until the parts were more important than the person. As the field developed, the error was corrected by Gestalt and personalistic psychologies that made the whole person greater than the sum of the parts. Holistic views of personality, built upon the premise of self-integrity, still prevail, particularly in counseling theory. For example, at the root of Carl Rogers's "client-centered therapy" is the principle that a personality has a natural desire for self-healing that needs to be stimulated and directed by the therapist. Likewise, educators have gone through cycles of moving pieces of "mental furniture" around in the minds of students until they are reminded that monsters are created out of mental giants and moral dwarfs. Executioners at Dachau were products of an educational system that permitted them to relax with a Beethoven symphony after a day at the ovens.

Neither can spiritual maturity be isolated from self-integrity. Jesus was far ahead of his time when he established this holistic principle for persons: "If your eye is sound [single], your whole body will be full of light" (Matt. 6:22). Contrary to some theological positions, the needs for self-preservation, self-actualization, and self-integrity are not sinful. At their physical and psychological origins, they are unconscious and amoral. Sooner or later, however, they will break through the borderline of awareness, seeking expression. When they do, volition will take over to direct their energies. Sin results when the conscious man twists the creative potential of these drives toward a selfish end at the expense of other persons and other goals. With this choice, the "will to live" (self-preservation) is reduced to survival, the "will to grow" (self-actualization) is snarled in egotism, and the "will to be whole" (self-integrity) is nothing more than the pieces of a lost dream. Christian conversion is the "turn-around" experience that sets in motion the creative forces for living abundantly, growing unselfishly, and becoming whole.

A MATURITY MODEL

Development toward our potential as persons and as Christians is not in conflict. If the psychological needs for self-preservation, self-actualization, and self-integrity are being constructively fulfilled, growth toward personal and Christian maturity results. As a framework for development, Harvard psychologist Gordon Allport established three criteria to measure maturity: (1) self-extension, (2) self-objectification, and (3) a unifying philosophy of life.[4]

By *self-extension*, Allport meant that the basic drives for self-preservation are principally governed by *psychogenic* rather than by *viscerogenic* needs.[5] Viscerogenic needs originate in the viscera ("guts"), that is, food, water, sleep, and sex. They tend to be self-centered and press for immediate gratification. Psychogenic needs are defined by social, intellectual, artistic, and spiritual interests. Generally, these needs require give-and-take with other persons and some form of deferred gratification. For instance, a team of medical scientists has worked more than twenty years on the research to isolate a cancer virus. Even though they are well paid, they must be willing to defer the demand for immediate gratification as professionals in favor of a longer-range and more significant goal. Self-extension is a characteristic of a mature person who has placed psychogenic above viscerogenic needs in his or her hierarchy of self-preservative interests.

Contrasting examples are all around us. Advocates of "do your own thing and do it now" must constantly raise the score for sensual satisfaction. "Tripping out" on alcohol, drugs, and sex brings immediate gratification and quick saturation. Satiated senses also spawn a boredom that drives the sensualist on an endless search for new experiences. Motion pictures are a self-condemning commentary on a sensual society. Having exhausted the exploration of alcoholism, movie makers have turned to drugs; having created boredom with hard-core heterosexual scenes, they shifted to homosexuality and then to perversion. Violence followed a similar pattern. After the public became inured to blood and guts, witchcraft, Satanism, and demon possession were made partners in a visual violence that had formerly been reserved for the confines of psychotic minds. A critic described a recent film by saying, "I thought that we had reached the bottom for bad taste and violence, but in this film, the bottom has fallen out." A day later, I asked a high school student if he had seen the film. "No," he answered, "but I feel as if I've seen it because that's all the kids are talking about." If deferring baser needs for higher, long-term values is characteristic of a mature person, our culture may be molding immaturity in future generations. At least, a self-extensive person will have to stand apart, if not alone.

Self-objectification is the second criterion that Allport as-
cribed to personal maturity. Socrates extolled this quality
in his dictum, "Know thyself." It means that a mature person lives without debilitating self-deception. In Allport's
words, self-objectification is ". . . that peculiar detachment
of the mature person when he surveys his own pretensions in
relation to his abilities, his present objectives in relation to
possible objectives for himself, his own equipment in comparison with the equipment of others, and his opinion of
himself in relation to the opinion others hold of him." [6]

Without self-objectification, a person will lean toward one
of two extremes: exaggerate his or her self-image by a false
show of power or compensate for the distortion by a false
show of humility. Either extreme signals immaturity. Mature persons have a realistic view of their personal assets
and liabilities. They can laugh at themselves and refrain
from judging others. Jesus put a treasure of psychological
nuggets into the warning, "Don't criticize people, and you
will not be criticized" (Matt. 7:1). More was meant than
the wisdom of avoiding retaliation. A person who criticizes
usually unveils more about himself or herself than about the
subject of the attack. Jesus was advancing self-objectification as one of the maturity goals for his followers.

Allport's third characteristic of personal maturity is a *unifying philosophy of life*. Self-extension and self-objectification must be integrated if they are to be meaningful. Otherwise, the psychogenic energies released by self-extension are
dissipated, and the personal insights resulting from self-
objectification are misdirected. According to Allport, a unifying philosophy of life is the staging area for the discipline
and direction of drives, needs, motives, and values in the
mature personality. Lacking this organizing center, immature
persons are victims of multiple loyalties, wasted energies,
and constant conflict.

Of course, it is possible for a person to have a unifying

philosophy of life that is totally self-centered. C. S. Lewis posed that idea by suggesting that a selfish person is happier than a Christian—in the short run.[7] When life is shaken out, however, selfishness creates a lonely hell within the narrow borders of an inflated ego.

Because the nerve center of spiritual maturity is a unifying philosophy of life, the concept deserves expansion. Allport says that a unifying philosophy of life should be well-differentiated, dynamic, productive, comprehensive, integral, and heuristic.[8]

A mature person has a wide range of *well-differentiated* responses. Some philosophies of life operate within a small radius. New situations create panic when they are outside the closed philosophical circle. Like Robinson Crusoe, security is limited to a beachhead, but danger begins at the edge of the jungle. In contrast, a well-differentiated world view permits a person to be "fully present" in many kinds of situations without compromising the principles of boundary conditions.

As a lesson in maturity, I compared my attention span at lengthy educational planning sessions with that of a senior-university president who stood out as a national leader. With my yellow legal pad in front of me, I wrote down items "To Be Done"—memos to administrators and daily correspondence. Snatches of the debate got through to me, and occasionally I'd turn a page to catch up with the reporting. Across the table sat the university president with more than ten times the students of my institution and twenty times the budget; yet he came to the meetings with his homework done, his place at the table clear, and his attention focused on the conversation. When he spoke, people listened, not just because he was powerful and experienced, but because he knew the subject at hand and had an opinion. As another of my mentors in the presidency, he taught me what it meant to be "fully present" with a well-differentiated philosophy of life.

Another feature of a unifying philosophy of life is its *dynamic* for action. A mature person is energized by his world view so that he repeatedly acts it out on the stage of daily behavior. During the Olympic games, commentators described Olga Korbut, a former gold medalist, as a twenty-one-year-old gymnast with the tired eyes of an ancient woman. How different from a seventy-nine-year-old professor of physics after whom we named our new science learning center. When his picture was engraved on a gold-anodized plate at the entrance to the building, I told the people at the dedication, "Look at the eyes." The hair was white, and the face was lined, but the eyes were youthfully bright with the future. Of course, Dr. Otto Miller followed the look in his eyes with action. Despite a bout with old age and cancer, he was a volunteer driver for the cancer society twice a week and a senior learner in a computer science course which he was taking to stay fresh in his field. Behind the dynamic of those eyes was a contagious commitment to Jesus Christ— the unifying center of his life.

A practical philosophy of life contains an element of faith— it is *heuristic*. No world view answers or anticipates all the questions of the universe. Therefore, a mature person holds his or her philosophy of life confidently but tentatively. By his own testimony, Paul made room for the unknown: "At present we are men looking at puzzling reflections in a mirror. The time will come when we shall see reality whole and face to face" (1 Cor. 13:12)! Jesus demonstrated heuristic faith when he admitted that the time of the coming of the Son of man was known only to the Father (see Acts 1:7). As Allport would say, "It is characteristic of the mature mind that it can act wholeheartedly even without absolute certainty." [9]

Ambiguity came as a shock to me when I was a junior in college. As the product of a home, church, and junior college where spiritual certainty reigned, I was unprepared for the intellectual bombardment of a professor in cultural anthropology. He deftly stripped away all the cultural layers of my faith and exposed an indefensible core. Confused and shaken, I could only pray, "God, if you exist and if there is anything to Christianity, show me now." Taking pity on my desperate state, God brought the person of Jesus Christ before my mind and rested his case. One might say that this was my intellectual conversion because I chose to do what Elton Trueblood described for me many years later: "A Christian is a person who is willing to bet his life that Christ is right." [19]

I returned to the class in cultural anthropology, and the earlier threat of relativism and ambiguity became the stimulus for a scholarly career as a committed Christian. Without pretending to set myself up as a mature model of Christian intellect, I started to learn how to live with Huston Smith's "fallibilism" and what Bernard Ramm has called "imponderables." Since then, I have been convinced that Christians should be on the frontiers of intellectual freedom because ambiguity is a challenge, not a threat. My humanistic psychologist friends must believe that the ultimate outcome of their research is the prediction and control of human behavior in order to come to a similar heuristic faith. Believers and nonbelievers can find maturity through a unifying philosophy of life, but the source and the degree of freedom is qualitatively different.

Finally, a unifying philosophy of life is *comprehensive*. By scope and penetration, every facet of human personality is gathered in—needs, motives, values, and goals. Holiness is a spiritual synonym for personal maturity. Immaturity is flawed by duplicity, polarity, and compartmentalization. Only in a mature person will you find the thread of a philosophy of life woven with integrity throughout the whole fabric of personality.

Dr. James F. Gregory, whom I've identified as my first mentor in the presidency, once said that "Be ye holy" meant to be comprehensively in the will of God. To illustrate, he pulled a loose thread from his suit coat, stretched it tight, and held it to the light, saying, "Take any thread from the fabric of your being and you will see that it has the full color and texture of the will of God."

THE TEMPTATION: A MATURITY TEST

As "The Event" in Jesus' life history, the temptation tested the maturity of his responses to the psychological needs for self-preservation, self-actualization, and self-integrity. Alone for forty days and nights, he also had to bring his newly awakened deity into the perspective of his full humanity. No one knows the issues he dealt with or the decisions he made during this period of preparation. Even though his identity may have been unfolding before him for years, the full awareness of being the Son of God would still be a shock. If so, Jesus may have spent the forty days working through the differences between his divine and human natures. Then, when his self-concept was intact, he turned to the strategy for his mission.

Meanwhile, Satan was biding his time. As the crafty master of temptation, he did not strike at the height of the spiritual experience; rather, he waited for the inevitable moment when elation subsided to attack his victim at the most vulnerable point. For Jesus, it was food. If he had entertained any illusions about his humanity during those mystical moments in communion with God, they were shattered by the first pang of hunger. Self-preservation was still a primary need for which there was no spiritual answer. Capitalizing on Jesus' "will to live," Satan made his move: "If you really are the Son of God, . . . tell these stones to turn into loaves [of bread]" (Matt. 4:3). A legitimate appeal to a natural desire is the most subtle snare for sin.

In a psychological context, Satan's proposal was the first

stage of a maturity test. Would Jesus live at a viscerogenic level and be dominated by physical drives with their demand for immediate gratification, or would he discipline those drives in order to live at the higher level of psychogenic interests? Would physical satisfactions be deferred for spiritual values? Would personal gratification give way to the needs of others? Self-extension was the quality of maturity under test.

If Jesus had turned the stones into bread, he would have made a laughing contradiction of his statement "the Son of Man himself has not come to be served but to serve, and to give his life to set many others free" (Mark 10:45). No convicting weight would be felt in his challenge "The man who tries to save his life will lose it; it is the man who loses his life for my sake and the Gospel's who will save it" (Mark 8:35).

Satan's strategy was sound. To strike at Jesus' will to live by provoking him to turn the stones into bread seemed innocent, but the devil had bigger stakes in mind. Later on, he would appeal again to Jesus' drive for self-preservation, only the next time the issue would be drawn on universal terms in the Garden of Gethsemane. Hunger was just a decoy for physical existence. Ultimately, Jesus would have to decide whether he would save his life for himself or give it in sacrifice for humankind. The temptation was an eternal morality play in microcosm. With us in mind, he answered resolutely, "The scripture says, 'Man shall not live by bread alone, but by every word that proceedeth out of the mouth of God'" (Matt. 4:4). His choice was made: spiritual values would take precedence over physical needs; gratification would be deferred; and self would be sacrificed for the needs of others.

Failure did not discourage the devil. Human nature has other psychological drives that put more than one arrow into his quiver. Transporting Jesus to the Holy City and lofting him to the highest ledge of the Temple, Satan sneered: "If you really are the Son of God, . . . throw yourself down from here, for the scripture says, *'He shall give his angels charge concerning thee, to guard thee,'* and *'On their hands they shall bear thee up, lest haply thou dash thy foot against a stone'* " (Luke 4:9–11).

Jesus' self-concept was under assault. "If you really are the Son of God" was a broadside against Jesus' human need for self-actualization. As with all of us, he wanted to *do good, do well,* and *be liked.* Could he withstand the temptation to prove his identity by a spectacular show of his authority as the Son of God? If he succumbed, he would short-circuit God's timing for the full revelation of his deity. Never would he be able to respond to those who flattered him, "My time has not come yet" (John 2:4). If he had given in to the temptation to prove his self-worth, Jesus would have repeated Adam's sin of preempting the will of God. His other choice was to accept the reality of his human limitations and contend:

> I assure you that the Son can do nothing of his own accord, but what he sees the Father doing. What the Son does is always modeled on what the Father does (John 5:19–20).

Knowing and accepting himself, Jesus refused to defend his ego with a miracle on his own behalf. This did not mean that he rolled over and played dead for Satan. Bringing his fighting spirit into the fray, he retorted, "Yes, [that's true, I am the Son of God] . . . and the scripture also says *'Thou shalt not tempt the Lord thy God'* " (Matt. 4:7). Jesus chose to redeem the world by obedience rather than to save himself by a *tour de force.*

With his decision, Jesus demonstrated self-objectification as an attribute of his maturity. Now he could summon his disciples to humility and call the Pharisees from their pride. Most important of all, Jesus had passed the preliminary test for the time when he would hear the same temptation, "If you are the son of God, step down from the cross" (Matt. 27:40). Once again, he would have to decide whether or not he would call the angels to his rescue. In the wilderness, the temptation was personal; on the cross, our future hung in the balance.

With consistent regularity, we have seen Jesus' maturity tied in with our destiny. Knowing himself, he had no need for self-deception or ego-defense. Therefore, his maturity works for our benefit as he extends beyond himself to obey God and love us.

Defeated twice, the devil took aim on Jesus' self-integrity for his *coup de grâce*. Showing him the magnificent kingdoms of the world, he hoped for a division of loyalty and a change of mission. If Jesus would just fall down and worship the devil, all the power, wealth, and status of the earth would be his. Of course, it would mean undoing thirty years of development and forty days of final preparation; so Satan gambled everything on the strategy of appealing to the power motive that resides in every human being. Was Jesus vulnerable to this temptation? We must remember that he was born in a manger, trained as a carpenter, and raised in a town that had a reputation for producing nothing good. Sociologists would label him a "disadvantaged person" who was condemned to political, economic, and cultural impoverishment. It would not be easy for Jesus to accept God's plan to remain poor and powerless.

A preacher once told about smugglers who tried to pay a ship's captain to carry contraband in his cargo. When the price was low, the captain adamantly refused to participate; but when the price was raised higher than the captain's earnings for a lifetime, he finally ordered, "Get off my boat. You're getting too close to my price!"

Assuming that every person has his or her price, the devil baited his disadvantaged prey with the power of the world.

Like the ship's captain, Jesus could mince no words. "Away with you, Satan! . . . the scripture says, '*Thou shalt worship the Lord thy God, and him only shalt thou serve* '" (Matt. 4:10). God would remain the organizing center and the unifying philosophy of life for Jesus. He was a whole man! From that time on, he claimed, "I am in the Father and the Father is in me . . . The man who has seen me has seen the Father" (John 14:10, 9).

Jesus' philosophy of life was practical as well as unifying. With a stake driven deeply into the will of God, the tether of his interests played out in a comprehensive and well-differentiated circle. He was at ease among children or scholars, fishermen or priests, revelers or ascetics, saints or sinners. His responses ranged from humor to judgment and from condemnation to mercy. Topics for his teaching stretched between love and hate, peace and war, life and death, freedom and determination. No stereotype could bind him except the consistency of his desire to do the will of God.

Energy is an outcome of a dynamic philosophy of life. After Jesus' visit with the woman at the well, the disciples returned from town with food and encouraged Jesus to eat. Never having been totally captivated by a dynamic sense of mission, they were baffled by the response, "My food is doing the will of him who sent me and finishing the work he has given me" (John 4:34).

The practicality of a philosophy of life is put to the acid test when a person has to live heuristically, or with unanswered questions. Despite his utter confidence in God, Jesus had to live with the "Grand Perhaps" that stalks the path of finite human beings. Part of Satan's temptation was to propose that Jesus trade an unseen future in God's hands for the visible kingdoms of the world. Jesus could have made that choice—at our expense. His submission would have given us no faith or hope beyond our own human efforts. With us in mind, Jesus made the mature decision.

76

Psychological analysis of the temptation is too cold. As one ventures vicariously into the experience, Jesus' excruciating agony in the final passion is presaged. Who knows the physical pain and mental exhaustion implied in the Gospel postscript of the temptation? "Then the devil left him alone, and angels came to him and took care of him" (Matt. 4:11). Maturity has its price, and Jesus paid the full measure.

As for the devil? Having "exhausted every kind of temptation, he withdrew until his next opportunity" (Luke 4:13). Human maturity is neither perfect nor static—and the devil knows it best.

Temptation confirmed that Jesus was a real, complete, and mature human being. He showed his followers that only the examined life is worth living. Jesus dashed the hopes of those who want freedom without discipline, growth without struggle, or faith without reason. He found freedom in obedience, growth in conflict, and faith in a philosophy of life.

The wilderness test puts a premium on adequate preparation for Christian witness. One wonders about "instant celebrities" who are created by conversion. When I heard Charles Colson speak just after his release from prison, his nervous chain-smoking and lapses into preconversion language established his spiritual authenticity with me. A few months later, I wept through his spiritual autobiography, *Born Again,* because I had already entered his struggle with him. But then, as he was vaulted into prominence as the "hottest" item on the evangelical Christian banquet circuit, I had second thoughts on his behalf. If Jesus needed forty days of prayerful reflection and a full-fledged test of his maturity before he entered the public arena, how much more time for growth and test should we provide someone whose earlier life contradicted Christianity? No fault rests with persons like Charles Colson. By some miracle of God's grace, they usually survive our failure to learn the lesson of timing for a public ministry from the Model of Jesus. Jesus might have entered the Temple to preach immediately after his baptism. He might have hammered out his values, worked through his identity, and pieced together his philosophy in the middle of a crowd; but, no, the needs of self had to be settled alone before he could serve. Otherwise he could not have survived when the temptation to turn stones into bread became a life-and-death matter in Gethsemane, when the pinnacle of the Temple became a cross, and when the promise of power became a palm leaf in the hands of well-intentioned people.

Ministers will readily recognize the seductive overtures in Satan's temptation of Jesus. Sooner or later, every person called of God must answer the question, What is the authority for my ministry? If the stones had been turned into bread, Jesus would have used miracles to answer that question. If he had thrown himself from the pinnacle of the Temple, he would have counted upon his image as the Son of God to sweep through his public ministry. If he had accepted Satan's offer of the kingdoms of the world, Jesus would have been able to minister in places of power and wealth but at the expense of the poor and the outcast.

Satan's temptations for ministers have not changed. With the subtlety of his serpenthood, he has victimized us with a ministerial hierarchy of success which puts miracle workers, image makers, and power brokers at the top. Underneath, he has created the temptations of envy, inadequacy, and imitation among ministers who cannot measure up.

As a Model for ministerial maturity, Jesus rejected Satan's hierarchy of success. Rather than relying upon miracles, he chose to be the servant of all; resisting the temptation to flaunt his image as the Son of God, he suffered through the struggles of human nature; refusing to negotiate for power, he cast his lot with the wretched of the earth. All our concepts of the ministry need to be reworked around the meaning of Jesus' ordination vow: "For the Son of Man himself has not come to be served but to serve, and to give his life to set many others free" (Matt. 20:28).

In the temptation, Satan intended to destroy his arch-enemy. Instead, Jesus turned pending disaster into a demonstration of his maturity. As "The Event" which cued his entrance onto the stage of human history, Jesus was now ready to put the imprint of his personality on his ideas and his ministry.

Chapter Five

HIS DISCIPLINE

DEITY DID NOT cover for Jesus' humanity. Just as he was subject to every temptation that comes to men and women, he had to exercise self-discipline over his human nature in order to remain free from sin. No special gift was conferred upon him because he was the Son of God or because he was filled with the Holy Spirit at baptism. Jesus entered the temptation with the same resources that are available to every common man or woman who seeks to do the will of God.

What were those resources? According to the Synoptic record, Jesus relied on the disciplines of *prayer, Scripture,* and *obedience.* Evidence before and after the experience shows that these tools of self-mastery were developed over a lifetime. No person could spend forty days fasting in the desert who had never prayed before; no carpenter could quote Scriptures to the devil unless they were accurately and spontaneously known; no vigorous human spirit who had never learned to obey could submit himself fully to God.

Even though the temptation was a watershed in Jesus' development, Satan only retreated temporarily, "biding his time" (Luke 4:13, NEB). Persistently, he baited Jesus with seductive traps until desperation led him to a frontal attack by pain and suffering. On none of these occasions did God intervene with supernatural forces to save his Son. Angels ministered to Jesus *after* he was tempted, but during the hours of stress, he had to stand alone. Only his strength as a disciplined man of prayer, Scripture, and obedience buffered him from sin. In the temptation, Jesus became more than a real and complete man who understands us; he also demonstrated that self-discipline is a prerequisite to maturity.

The Discipline of Prayer

Interpretations of prayer range from a humanistic view of psychological reinforcement to the overspiritualized idea of supernatural transference. As a discipline in the life of Jesus, neither extreme fits. For him, the purpose of prayer was *fellowship* with the Father, *guidance* for personal decisions, and *preparation* for life situations. As such, prayer had to be developed as a continuous and pervasive pattern of behavvior—the constant awareness of the presence of God.

Jesus' public and private prayers run like a thread through the Gospels from his first prayer at the baptism (see Luke 3:21) to his last plea for his enemies on the cross (see Luke 28:34). He prayed in the morning (see Mark 1:35), in the evening (see Mark 6:47), and on one occasion, all night long (see Luke 6:12). But conclusive evidence of prayer as a habit of Jesus is given almost inadvertently by Luke. With suspense thickening in the plot against his master, Luke observed:

> Then he went out of the city and up onto the Mount of Olives, *as he had often done before,* with the disciples fol-

lowing him. And when he reached his *usual* place, he said
to them,
"Pray that you may not have to face temptation!" (Luke
22:39–40, italics mine).

A habit that becomes a drive (Allport's "functional auton-
omy") is fundamental to the development of a discipline; so
Jesus prayed "often" and in a "usual" place.

No special virtue is guaranteed by the habit of prayer.
Content tells more than frequency. Jesus depended on prayer
for a continuing perspective of his role and mission. Or, stated
in psychological terms, prayer was a self-extending, self-
objectifying, and self-unifying experience. Specific examples
confirm prayer as an *instrument of clarification and confirma-
tion* in the development of Jesus.

Then came this incident. While Jesus was praying by himself, having only the disciples near him, he asked them this
question:
"Who are the crowd saying that I am?" (Luke 9:18).

By inference, the subject of Jesus' prayer was his dual
identity. Whether struggling with self-doubts, impatient with
his humanity, or assessing the effectiveness of his teaching,
he needed a reality check on people's perception of his nature. Perhaps the question had been prompted by the miracle of the feeding of the five thousand that had just taken
place. He may have wanted to compare the outcomes of working wonders among the masses with the teaching of concepts
to a small group of disciples. Whatever his motive, the answer of the crowd through the lips of the disciples was obvious.

"Some say that you are John the Baptist," they replied.
"Others that you are Elijah, and others think that one of the
old-time prophets has come to life again" (Luke 9:19).

A faith created by miracles needs other miracles to sustain

it! Jesus knew then that he could not build his kingdom on a milk-fed faith; so he turned the quiz back to his disciples:

"And who do you say that I am?"
"God's Christ!" said Peter (Luke 9:20).

From that time on, Jesus became more suspicious of the motives of crowds and gave more time to teaching his disciples. In prayer, the original question came into focus.

Students of administrative theory will be intrigued by Jesus' use of prayer in the *decision-making process.* Of all executive responsibilities, none is more crucial than staff selection, particularly in situations where leadership must eventually be transferred from the founder of the movement to his or her disciples. Leadership choices then must reflect skill in foreseeing the potential development as well as the present ability of persons. In preparation for selecting his staff, Jesus sought counsel:

It was in those days that he went up the hillside to pray, and *spent the whole night in prayer to God.* When daylight came, he summoned his disciples to him and out of them he chose twelve whom he called apostles (Luke 6:12–13, italics mine).

No other decision or event in Jesus' life is preceded by an explicit scriptural reference to a "whole night in prayer to God." An uncanny "sense of the significant" brought him to his knees to ask God's help in sorting and selecting future leadership for the kingdom of God.

Prayer is expected in a time of decision but not in a moment of glory. A millionaire businessman pointed out to me his only investment that wasn't paying a profit and jokingly said, "I told the Lord that those condominiums were his and if he wanted me to give a gift to the church it was up to him to make them pay." Prayer is often approached the same way.

Emergencies and failures belong to God, but we claim the credit for success.

Jesus took the opposite view. He prayed *before* emergencies and *after* success. For instance, one sermon and one miracle carried his reputation like a wild fire when he began his ministry (see Mark 1:28). The next day, everyone was looking for him; so Jesus got up before the dawn and went to a deserted place to pray. From that time on, his efforts to avoid public acclaim failed, and prayer became his only respite.

> Yet the news about him spread all the more, and enormous crowds collected to hear Jesus and to be healed of their diseases. *But he slipped quietly away to deserted places for prayer* (Luke 5:15–16, italics mine).

Eventually the rising tide of popularity peaked, and the crowds tried to force a crown upon the head of their miracle worker. "Then Jesus, realizing that they were going to carry him off and make him their king, retired once more to the hillside quite alone" (John 6:15).

A hillside may have been for hiding, but in the pattern of a lifetime, it also was a place of prayer for Jesus.

With each accolade of the crowd, Satan's glamorous vision of all the wealth and power of the kingdoms of the world must have been rerun before Jesus' eyes. In the wilderness, the temptation was hypothetical, but in a horde of people, the slightest gesture of encouragement would have set in motion forces that not even Jesus could reverse. One can imagine a deerlike fright in his eyes as he saw the danger of a "flash point" in the milling masses. Physical flight took him to a place of prayer where he could regain the perspective that his time had not yet come. Away from the whirl and the rhythm of the crowd, Jesus found in prayer the objectivity to resort his priorities and pull straying motives back into the singular purpose of his life.

Intensity characterized the prayer of Jesus when *crisis*

loomed. In the Garden of Gethsemane, every facet of his being was behind the petition for relief from the cup of suffering. Luke made this diagnosis as a physician: "He was in agony and prayed even more intensely so that his sweat was like great drops of blood falling to the ground" (Luke 22:44).

Physical needs, psychological motives, and spiritual values were at stake in the Garden just as they had been in the temptation. As a link between the two experiences, Jesus repeated his prayer three times.

> "Dear Father," he said, "all things are possible to you. Please—let me not have to drink this cup! Yet it is not what I want but what you want" (Mark 14:36).

Utter obedience in the Garden was the antecedent of total temptation in the wilderness. Both engaged three basic human needs: self-preservation, self-actualization, and self-integrity. The focus, however, had shifted from the devil's external attack to Jesus' inner struggle with his own will. Would he lay down his vibrant desire to live and be willing to die prematurely? Would he sacrifice his confident self-image and accept a criminal's disgrace? Would he self-destruct his tuned integrity and be forsaken by his Father?

Each question shook out into a single decision: Would Jesus lose his will in the will of God? Three times he prayed, and three times he submitted himself to the priority of God's purpose. Even though he had cultivated the discipline of prayer over a lifetime, he had not anticipated the conflict that would burst out in the agony: "My heart is nearly breaking" (Mark 14:34). Intense prayer settled the issue.

Against the background of a disciplined life of prayer, Jesus responded to his disciples' request, "Lord, teach us how to pray" (Luke 11:1), with a model for them to follow. Appropriately, it is called the Lord's Prayer because it is also a mirror in which we see Jesus reflecting upon the meaning of the discipline in his own experience.

The Lord's Prayer (Matt. 6:9–13, KJV)	*Jesus' Experience*
Our Father	Jesus didn't have to reintroduce himself to God. A salutation of natural affection assumes continuous fellowship and full obedience between formal prayers. "If you keep my commandments you will live in my love just as I have kept my Father's commandments and live in his love" (John 15:10).
which art in heaven, Hallowed be thy name.	Acknowledging the humanity that he shared with his disciples, Jesus identified God as transcendent and holy—the self-objectifying source against which he gained the perspective of his own image and value. "I assure you that the Son can do nothing of his own accord, but only what he sees the Father doing" (John 5:19).
Thy kingdom come. Thy will be done in earth, as *it is* in heaven.	Reflecting upon the unifying philosophy of his life, Jesus recalled his need for continuous reinforcement of the decision to lose his self-consciousness in the consciousness of God and implement that decision by an open commitment to whatever role and mission God might assign to him. ". . . yet it must not be what I want, but what you want" (Matt. 26:39).

86

The Lord's Prayer	*Jesus' Experience*

Give us this day our daily bread.

Perhaps the temptation still occupied Jesus' mind as he remembered that hunger was the basic need through which the devil launched his attack. If, therefore, his disciples declared their dependence upon God to meet physical needs, they could extend themselves to concentrate on higher values.

"Set your heart on his kingdom and his goodness, and all these things will come to you as a matter of course" (Matt. 6:33).

And forgive us our debts, as we forgive our debtors.

Jesus knew that human relationships are interlocked in two dimensions: God-to-man and man-to-man. Although he did not sin himself, he was both observer and victim of a broken relationship because of selfishness. Putting himself into the breach between God and man, he proposed that forgiveness was the means for healing and that it is only effective when applied in both dimensions.

"And whenever you stand praying, you must forgive anything that you are holding against anyone else, and your Heavenly Father will forgive you *your* sins (Mark 11:25).

And lead us not into temptation, but deliver us from evil:

Perhaps recalling that the Spirit led him into the wilderness where he was tempted, Jesus wanted to spare his disciples the anguish of total temptation at the outer limits of human nature. He also foresaw the suffering of the cross—a situation created by environmental factors with which he could not cope unless God intervened. Knowing that his disciples would be confronted with similar situations, he approved a petition for escape or rescue.

"Dear Father," he said, "all things are possible to you. Please—let me not have to drink this cup!" (Mark 14:36).

For thine is the kingdom, and the power, and the glory, for ever. Amen.

As Jesus opened his prayer with familiar words of communion with the Father, he closed with the oft-repeated confidence that God has ultimate control over the resources to answer prayer and would be honored by the results.

"Jesus looked steadily at them and replied, 'Humanly speaking it is impossible; but with God anything is possible!'" (Matt. 19:26).

By his example and teaching, Jesus commended the discipline of prayer to us as a human resource for maintaining fellowship with God, for gaining perspective on personal decisions, and for preparing for situations that test our commitment. Effectively developed, prayer is the means for implementing the resolution to follow Christ by continuously setting the boundaries and providing the energy for growth toward our human potential in the will of God.

THE DISCIPLINE OF SCRIPTURE

Prayer is a subjective discipline that needs to be balanced by the objectivity of an external authority. For Jesus, the Holy Scriptures were the Word of God and his command. The product of a devout Jewish home, Jesus memorized the

Old Testament from earliest childhood and undoubtedly continued the discipline through his life. People who had known him as a boy in the neighborhood were astounded by his ability to teach the Scriptures in the synagogue, and strangers exclaimed, "No man ever spoke like that!" (John 7:46), after Jesus quoted, "The man who believes in me . . . will have rivers of living water flowing from his inmost heart" (John 7:38).

One of the aspects of the discipline of Scripture was Jesus' decision to obey the Word of God rather than the tradition of men. Using the authority of Scripture itself as the basis for discernment, Jesus said:

> You hypocrites, Isaiah described you beautifully when he wrote—
>
> > This people honoureth me with their lips,
> > But their heart is far from me.
> > But in vain do they worship me,
> > Teaching as doctrines the precepts of men.
>
> You are so busy holding on to the traditions of men that you let go the commandment of God! (Mark 7:6–8).

By adopting the Scriptures as the sole authority for his life, Jesus believed in their *divine inspiration, historical accuracy,* and *eternal value.* Time and again, he attested his conviction about the inspired truth of the Word of God with the preface, "It stands written" (Matt. 26:31, NEB). Going even further, he made it clear that the Scriptures also took on the authority of historical accuracy: "Indeed, I assure you that, while Heaven and earth last, the Law will not lose a single dot or comma until its purpose is complete" (Matt. 5:18).

Toward the close of his ministry, Jesus' preaching took on an apocalyptic tone as he predicted the end of time. But against the impermanence of all creation, he compared the

Scriptures: "Earth and sky will pass away, but my words will never pass away" (Matt. 24:35).

The impact of the discipline of the Scriptures upon Jesus' life can be inferred by extension. He said that his own words were the fulfillment of the Old Testament revelation and that they carried the same authority and power. So when Jesus said that his words "pruned" the vine to produce growth and fruit, he must have been speaking from his encounters with the Old Testament (see John 12:37–50). Also he dared to put up his words as a standard of judgment for the decisions of men: "Every man who rejects me and will not accept my sayings has a judge—at the last day, the very words that I have spoken will be his judge" (John 12:48).

Yet all is not negative in the authority of Jesus' words. At the time he claimed his oneness with the Father before Jewish scholars, he revealed the ultimate purpose of the Word of God:

> You pore over the scriptures, for you imagine that you will find *eternal life* in them. And all the time they give their testimony to me (John 5:39, italics mine).

As Jesus projected the value of his words for his disciples, he was witnessing to the impact of the Scriptures in his own development. To him, the Word of God was the *pruning instrument* to prepare for growth and effectiveness, the *final standard of judgment* for belief and behavior, and the *source of eternal life*.

With the objectivity of divine revelation and the evidence of personal impact, Jesus took his confidence in the authority of Scriptures into temptation, teaching, and debate. Holy Scripture was the only counterweapon Jesus used against the devil's attack on his humanity. If he had responded with his own resources of logic, will power, or anger, he would have fallen. Humanity, however strong or good, is never a match for the forces of evil. Only the Word of God has the authority to resist the power of Satan; so when Jesus responded to the tempting offers, he did not inject a single word of personal interpretation into the scriptural reference. Forcefully he said, "It stands written," and then quoted the rebuttal. Once beaten, the devil used the most devious ploy of all: he twisted Scripture itself into temptation. " 'If you are the Son of God,' he said, throw yourself down from here, for the scripture says, *"He shall give his angels charge concerning thee, to guard thee,"* and *"On their hands they shall bear thee up, lest haply thou dash thy foot against a stone'"* (Luke 4:9–11).

Rather than debating the truth which had been turned against him, Jesus closed the conversation with the categorical rejection, "It is also said, *'Thou shalt not tempt the Lord thy God'"* (Luke 4:12).

The lesson is humbling, if not embarrassing. Jesus, a real and complete man, proved that the discipline of Scripture is the only counterauthority with which we can resist the temptation to sin in our human nature. The resource is still readily available through discipline.

The Discipline of Obedience

Obedience is a complementary resource to prayer and Scripture. There is a sense, however, in which Jesus' obedience stood apart as a separate discipline. ". . . Son though he was, he had to *prove* the meaning of obedience through *all* that he *suffered*" (Heb. 5:8, italics mine).

The weight of these words informs us that Jesus developed obedience through the taxing grind of the human proving ground. Every aspect of his life was absorbed in the trial, and no results were known without suffering.

At a fundamental level, Jesus learned obedience through self-denial. He fasted for forty days in the desert (see Luke 4:2), established principles of fasting in his preaching (see

Matt. 6:16–18), and warned his disciples, "Be on your guard
—see to it that your minds are never clouded by dissipation
or drunkenness or the worries of this life, or else that day
may catch you like the springing of a trap" (Luke 21:34).

Earlier I noted that Jesus mentioned self-denial as one
option for handling the sex drive outside marriage (see Matt.
19:12). The inference is that he spoke from experience.
Self-denial runs the danger of degenerating into ascetic pride
or a call for sympathy. It needs to be lifted to the higher
motive which Jesus learned to obey. With full knowledge
that he was heading for the suffering of the cross, Jesus told
his disciples, "I go on my way to show the world that I *love*
the Father and *do* what he sent me to do. . . . Get up now!
Let us leave this place" (John 14:31, italics mine).

Love, not asceticism, motivated Jesus to obey. Rather than
being drawn to self-denial for a negative or neurotic reason,
he was willing to defer gratification of human needs in order
to gain a higher value. "For he himself endured a cross and
thought nothing of its shame because of the *joy* he knew
would follow his suffering" (Heb. 12:2).

In this case, joy was a long-term goal that made suffering
worthwhile, but not all of the rewards of obedience are so
distant. Jesus promised admission to a *family relationship*
for anyone who obeyed him: "For whoever does the will of
my Heavenly Father is brother and sister and mother to me"
(Matt. 12:50).

Another immediate return for the discipline of obedience
is *spiritual discernment*. At the height of the Feast of the
Tabernacles in Jerusalem, Jesus went to the Temple to
teach. His knowledge amazed the Jews who asked, "How
does this man know all this—he has never been taught?"
(John 7:15). Jesus replied:

> My teaching is not really mine but comes from the one who
> sent me. If anyone wants to do God's will, *he will know*

whether my teaching is from God or whether I merely speak on my own authority" (John 7:16–17, italics mine).

To fellowship and knowledge, then, is added the most rewarding benefit of all—the *continuous presence* of the Spirit of God in Christ. During a teaching seminar with the disciples, Judas (not Iscariot) asked Jesus how he could make himself known to them but not to the world at the same time. His answer was:

> When a man loves me, he follows my teaching. Then my Father will love him, and we will come to that man and *make our home within him* (John 14:23, italics mine).

When the benefits are compared with the cost of obedience, Jesus proved that the discipline is worth learning, even in suffering.

Reluctance still surrounds the thought of Jesus' blundering through the trial-and-error experiences of our humanity until he learns the lesson of obedience. Does this mean that the weight of his humanity pulled down on him like it does on us? Did he ever feel as if he were on a treadmill making no progress? Did he suffer the limitations of his nature as well as the restrictions of his environment? Yes, all these elements were part of his obedience test. Like us, he had to work to commit his humanity to the larger purpose of God and to live by the commandments rather than by the self-centered needs of human nature. All this was boot-camp training for the moment when God asked him for obedience that was without "return, regret, or reservation" in the Garden of Gethsemane. By a disciplined affirmative, Jesus reversed the self-preservation principle and made self-denial a life-saving feature of the gospel:

> "If anyone wants to follow in my footsteps, he must give up all right to himself, take up his cross and follow me. The man who tries to save his life will lose it; it is the man who

loses his life for my sake and the gospel's who will save it" (Mark 8:34–35).

Prayer for inner direction, *Scripture* for external authority, and *obedience* for human fulfillment were the resources that Jesus had to match his humanity. Developing them through discipline, he showed how the same resources are available to us. Will we take Peter's advice to "follow in his steps" until we have Paul's confidence, "Copy me, my brothers, as I copy Christ himself"?

Part Three

THE PSYCHOLOGY OF JESUS

*"He did not need anyone to tell him what people were like:
he understood human nature."*

John 2:25

Chapter Six

PRINCIPLES OF PERSONHOOD

JESUS WAS a serious student of human behavior. Shortly after the opening of his ministry, a groundswell of public opinion arose in his favor. Looking back to the temptation and forward to the cross, Jesus saw the fleeting nature of fame. According to John's Gospel, "He did not need anyone to tell him what people were like: he understood human nature" (John 2:25).

Divine insight alone cannot account for Jesus' knowledge of people. With the advantage of natural development and total temptation, Jesus learned the meaning of his own motives, needs, and goals. Personal experience and practical insight, therefore, became the substance out of which he fashioned working principles of personhood. None was written in textbook terms, but all were proven in human relationships. From the scriptural record, Jesus preached and proved the *worth, uniqueness,* and *unity* of persons.

THE WORTH OF A PERSON

Individual worth was a radical message for the world in which Jesus lived. The Roman Empire was built on the backs of sixty million slaves. Its "Super Bowl" was the Colosseum where the difference between life and death depended on a turn of the emperor's thumb. Despite the Roman code of justice, the father of a newborn child had the irrevocable authority of *patria potestas*—to decide whether the baby was to be kept or thrown into the streets.

Against Rome's capricious system of pricing persons, the Jews fiercely defended the value of the human spirit. David, their king and poet, had left them a song of creation:

> When I consider thy heavens, the work of thy fingers, the moon and the stars, which thou hast ordained;
> What is man, that thou art mindful of him? and the son of man, that thou visitest him?
> For thou hast made him a little lower than the angels, and hast crowned him with glory and honour.
> Thou madest him to have dominion over the works of thy hands; thou hast put all things under his feet (Ps. 8:3–6, KJV).

Jesus shared his people's conviction that a person had infinite worth and a privileged position in the universe because he or she was created in the image of God. Jewish theology, however, was better than its practice. Personal worth was weighed on a scale of ethnic religion with the highest value given to a pure Hebrew strain. Half-breeds, like the Samaritans, were equal to "dogs."

In his first sermon, Jesus refuted the Roman view of persons and restored the Jewish meaning of creation. He preached to a motley crowd of disenfranchised people:

> Two sparrows sell for a penny, don't they? Yet not a single sparrow falls to the ground without your Father's knowledge. The very hairs of your head are all numbered. Never be afraid, then—you are far more valuable than sparrows (Matt. 10:29–31).

With one sermonic stroke, Jesus sounded a note of hope in an age when persons were devalued commodities on a surplus market. Whether in dealing with religious dignitaries or social outcasts, he never reneged on the principle that persons have value.

A distinction must be made between the intrinsic worth and the inherent goodness of a person. Although "original sin" is a theological concept, it has specific implications for a psychology of personality. If a person is inherently good, his or her worth is based on his or her goodness. If one assumes this is true, religion and psychology would share the common goal of setting a person free from the environmental circumstances that thwart his or her goodness. Many criminologists, educators, and politicians embrace this notion. At the recent retirement of one of the nation's most distinguished university presidents, his greatness was attributed to the fact that he never faltered in his belief that human nature was perfectible through education. He was motivated by the doctrine of human goodness. Others use the same doctrine as an excuse.

A mugger who beat his victim to death in Central Park plead "not guilty" at his trial even though he had confessed the crime. His attorneys argued that he was not responsible for the act because our society had produced the ghetto where he lived and learned only the law of survival in the concrete jungle. Carried to its extreme, the doctrine of inherent goodness is a companion of environmental determinism and a "no-fault" society.

Jesus is an excess piece of historical baggage if human nature is inherently good. God had already given enough examples of men and women who were saintly despite their circumstances. But what if David's confession is universal? "Behold, I was shapen in iniquity; and in sin did my mother conceive me" (Ps. 51:5, KJV). Inherent goodness is no longer the reason for our worth; and if personal goodness is a possibility, human nature will have to be changed. The potential for goodness, not moral inheritance or status, is the foundation for the worth of a person.

Karl Menninger has a grip on this truth in his book *Whatever Became of Sin?* After critically examining the attempts to reduce sin to a psychological, social, or legal problem, he compares our optimism about human nature to a bluebird singing on a dung-heap. For a remedy, he puts the voice of thunder in the mouths of ministers:

> What shall we cry? Cry comfort, cry repentance, cry hope. Because recognition of our part in the world transgression is the only remaining hope.[1]

Jesus accepted the fact that men and women are born in sin and still saw in them the higher purpose for which they were created. Otherwise, he would not have spent most of his time with rejects! In them, the potential for goodness could be dramatically displayed. An oft-cited example is Jesus' attitude toward children. Roman prejudice had rubbed off on the disciples, who tried to keep noisy youngsters away from the Master. They were sternly rebuked:

> You must let little children come to me, and you must never prevent their coming. The kingdom of Heaven belongs to little children like these. I tell you, the man who will not accept the kingdom of God like a little child will never get into it at all (Luke 18:16–17).

Today the value of a child has been markedly increased under the influence of developmental psychology and humanitarian movements. How different it was in Jesus' day to cut across the grain of prevailing values in defense of little people! At risk, he even used a child to illustrate his general principle about the infinite worth of an individual.

> What do you think? If a man has a hundred sheep and one wanders away from the rest, won't he leave the ninety-nine on the hillside and set out to look for the one who has wandered away? Yes, and if he should chance to find it I assure you he is more delighted over that one than he is over the ninety-nine who never wandered away. You can understand then that it is never the will of your Father in Heaven that a single one of these little ones should be lost (Matt. 18:12–14).

No doubt can remain that persons, however small or sinful, are priceless to Jesus.

A legend has grown up around the artistry of Michelangelo. Before he had fame or patrons, he foraged in a marble dump for the cast-off pieces of master sculptures. In his search, he claimed that he could see the angel form in a rejected rock. As a sculptor, his task was simply to free the form by chipping away the prison of excess marble. Even the *Pieta,* his most magnificent creation, is reputed to be the product of a rejected stone.

Artistry with rejects is the beauty of Jesus' relationships with people. Whether it was a noisy child, an adulterous woman, a haughty scribe, or a chained psychotic, he foresaw their worth and fashioned their wholeness as persons.

THE UNIQUENESS OF A PERSON

One of Jesus' most familiar stories is the parable of the talents. Apart from its timeless spiritual value, the parable outlines a principle of individual differences that ". . . predates the intelligence test by many centuries." [2] This principle is usually missed because emphasis is placed on the outcome of the story—individual responsibility for natural assets. Equally important is the fact that the talents were distributed to the recipients, "according to their respective abilities" (Matt. 25:15). Rather than pouring all persons into the same mold, the parable presupposes an infinite range of individual capacity and achievement.

Psychology is still trying to catch up with Jesus' principle of individual differences. After more than a century of searching for the commonalities in human personality, differential psychology is developing on the front edge of the field. Rather than dividing persons into parts or adding up the pieces for generalizations about the total personality, the emphasis is on the factors that account for individual variation. Textbooks in differential psychology should reserve a section for credits to the teaching of Jesus!

An extension of the parable of the talents is found in the parable of the sower. Individuality is still the subject, but the accent has shifted from ability to receptivity. Using the analogy of different kinds of soil to represent individual variation, Jesus spoke a simple truth. Each person is a unique environment in which his or her receptivity to the Gospel (the seed) is conditioned by his or her total learning experience (the soil). In addition, an individual's readiness to respond is related to the characteristics of personal maturity —self-extension, self-objectification, and a unifying philosophy of life. Four levels of receptivity and response are identified among the hearers of the Gospel.

The *Wayside Hearer* listens to the Word but does not accept its meaning. "Thoughtlessness, spiritual stupidity, arising not so much from want of intellectual capacity as from preoccupation of mind, is the characteristic of the first class." [3] While the exact reason for preoccupation is unknown, the superficiality of the response suggests that the individual was a captive of baser, visceral drives. His mind had been beaten hard by the compulsive demands for immediate self-gratification. Baked in this mode by habit, a shallow moral response is the best that can be mustered.

During my experience as a hospital chaplain, I frequently encountered persons who had a lifetime of selfish choices. They were prime candidates for death-bed conversions during the three-day life-and-death cycle after major surgery. As a rule of thumb, the third day was the slough of physical and spiritual despond. Patients were convinced that they were dying and that they had to make amends. Sensualists were the first to respond and the first to forget. As soon as the body began to heal, attention shifted from survival to pleasure again. After several disappointments, I joined other hospital chaplains who are generally pessimistic about death-bed conversions.

Wayside Hearers are immature personalities who have drawn a tight circle around their ego needs. Consequently, they are poor candidates for the self-extensive requirements of the gospel. Their selfish habits have become drives so that the invasion of spiritual values would pry loose their tenuous hold on whatever personal integrity exists in a visceral person. New insight would be a trauma that would leave them without defense. Jesus talked about spiritual values; Wayside Hearers live for selfish needs.

The *Stony-Ground Hearer* listens to the Word and enthusiastically receives it. Excitability always surrounds new insight. Later on, when the implications of truth require changes in motives, habits, and goals, the shock of recognition leads to rejection.

Willie Loman and Rabbit Redux are nonheroes of superficiality in contemporary literature. Each responded quickly to the initial challenge of personal insight but lacked the moral fiber to turn good intentions into a new life. Martin Luther once described the miracle chasers of Jesus' time as members of a "milk-fed" faith. As long as they saw miracles, they believed. Without the reinforcement of the sensational, they lapsed into skepticism or were led into hostility.

Perhaps under the sway of mob rhythm, Stony-Ground Hearers respond joyfully to the gospel, or perhaps they savor the variety of any novelty that breaks the monotony of routine. Whatever the case, their insight fluctuates with their feelings. They are immature because they do not know themselves. Lacking the depth of self-objectification, their behavior is buffeted by the impulse of the moment. To them, the gospel is just another crosswind among competing gusts that will be blown away before its personal implications can be absorbed. What a tragic picture! Their intellectual and volitional roots remain dormant and untouched by the fleeting fervor of faith. In *The Parabolic Teaching of Christ*, Alexander Bruce said that the Stony-Ground Hearer's "root is in others, in a prevalent popular enthusiasm; his religion is a thing of sympathetic imitation." [4] In quiet moments, Stony-Ground Hearers might wish otherwise, but a life-long pattern has made them incapable of the self-knowledge the gospel requires of human personality.

The *Thorn-Choked Hearer* listens to the Word and is ready to accept it as a changing force in life. Not trapped by the shallowness of the Wayside Hearer or the sightlessness of the Stony-Ground Hearer, the Thorn-Choked Hearer has the potential for maturity. Self-extensive interests and self-objectifying knowledge have been absorbed as agents of change in his or her personality; yet this individual lacks one element essential to maturity. Conflicting loyalties divide his or her attention. As a "double-souled man," this person does not have a unifying philosophy of life. Jesus called a man like this to follow him one day. The answer came back, "I am going to follow you, Lord, *but first* let me bid farewell to my people at home" (Luke 9:61, italics mine). Two desires of equal value vied for his loyalty. Rather than choosing one or the other, he remained ambivalent—"in between two minds." [5] By not making a choice, he eliminated the possibility of full maturity.

In the movie version of Lloyd Douglas's classic novel *Magnificent Obsession,* the senior physician tells his promising but wandering protégé, "Someday you will find an obsession; and when you do, it will be magnificent!" As in the Thorn-Choked Hearer, maturity is quiescent in persons who hold high values and live with a minimum of pretense. They only need a singular, compelling motive around which to organize their lives and sort out their priorities in order to be effective persons.

The *Fruitful Hearer* listens to the Word, receives it, and puts it into action. Timing is all important. Like a child who comes to the "golden moment" of readiness to learn, the Fruitful Hearer possesses all the growth lines for maturity, and they have converged. He or she is ready to rise above selfish interests, accept limitations, and seek a cause to which he or she can give his or her life. The growth rate is phenomenal. "As for the seed sown on good soil, this means the men who hear the message and accept it and do produce a crop—thirty, sixty, even a hundred times as much as they received" (Mark 4:20).

Effective behavior is the performance goal of personal maturity. Jesus declared that he would preach to the poor, proclaim release to the captives, restore the sight of the blind, set free the bruised, and announce the acceptable year of the Lord (see Luke 4:18–19). All the rest of the Gospel record gives evidence of his effectiveness in achieving these goals. By Jesus' example, a mature Christian also can be effective although productivity is not an end in itself. Movement toward maturity has the ongoing benefits of satisfaction in self-giving service and a sense of humor to balance self-importance. Above all, Jesus' promise of "far more life than before" (John 10:10) awaits a person who comes under the motivating power of a unifying philosophy of life.

The parable of the sower is not intended to pigeonhole persons. Differences of receptivity and response are used to represent Jesus' recognition that individuals are unique. In his day, rigid lines of ethnic and social status left little room for variation. By responding to persons rather than to roles, he brought the breeze of a liberating spirit to human relationships.

THE UNITY OF A PERSON

Theoretically, almost everyone agrees that a person is a unit in which the whole is greater than the sum of the parts. Practice belies our theory. We often dissect people and respond only to the parts. Toffler, of *Future Shock* fame, condemns contemporary society for the development of "modular men." [6] He means that persons are defined by their specialization so that human relationships become temporary and interchangeable modules that are plugged in or out as the situation demands. For instance, a university presidency is a specialized role to which people respond with deference, indifference, and hostility. The role is only a modular part of the total person who holds the office; yet that is the segment to which people respond. Students voice this dilemma when they say, "We want to know the person as well as the president."

As society becomes more complex and roles become more specialized, Toffler envisions further fragmentation of persons. A shock wave of the future may be massive systems of human interaction in which only parts of people are involved as they momentarily serve us or we serve them. If so, treacherous substitutes for unified people may be sought by artificial or exotic means, that is, by dictators or drugs.

Fragmentation took a different form in Jesus' day. Philosophy, under the influence of Plato, had dichotomized human nature into the bad flesh and good spirit. Nations had divided their subjects into citizens and slaves. Religionists, such as the Pharisees, had separated the letter from the spirit of the Law. All of them missed the meaning of a person as an entity.

Jesus put people back together again—physically, psychologically, and spiritually. Mind and body were assumed to be interdependent when Jesus asked the lame man at the Pool of Bethesda, "Do you want to get well again?" The inference was that the man was also psychologically crippled. Jesus had to know if he was as emotionally ready for healing as he was physically needy. An affirmative answer came back; so Jesus engaged him in a mutual act of physical healing with the command, "Get up." Then he said, "Do not sin again" (see John 5:6–14). Body, mind, and soul were one.

Time and again, Jesus made it known that persons cannot sin, be hurt, or be healed in parts. On one occasion, he quizzed the Pharisees, "Which do you suppose is easier—to say to a paralyzed man, 'Your sins are forgiven,' or 'Get up, pick up your bed and walk'?" (Mark 2:9–10). To him, a person is like an ecological system in which each part affects the whole. To heal a person's illness without forgiving his or her sins would violate the principle that defined the essence of the gospel: "Thou shalt love the Lord thy God with all thy heart and with all thy soul and with all thy strength and with all thy mind—and thy neighbor as thyself." (Luke 10:27). No part of a person was neglected. "Heart, soul, strength, and mind" encompass the affective, volitional, and cognitive components of personality. With a single focus on the will of God, Jesus made it clear that the potential for wholeness begins with the entire person.

A freshman with steel eyes and a stone face was ushered into my office one day. All the processes of discipline and the patience of the disciplinarians had been exhausted on him. Expulsion from the institution seemed to be the only recourse; so the president's office was the court of last resort. I began by reviewing a sordid history of violations that involved every area of campus life. In response, he erupted with a tirade of hate and profanity, which ended only when he stood and defiantly threatened, "I'm leaving, and you'll never see me again."

Contrary to my nature, I remained calm and answered, "Larry, you may walk out if you choose, but before you do, ask yourself whether this is the decision you would still want to make ten years from now." Never have I spoken so few words with such force. He froze in shock, crumpled into the chair, and began to weep convulsively. Two hours later, a redeemed man shook my hand and left the office to try again.

At the end of that year, a professor brought in a "Life Aims" paper that the same freshman had written for a psychology class. The turnaround was complete. His grades were beginning to reflect his intellectual ability; he was starring on the track team; his probation in the residence hall had been lifted; and he was anticipating a major in special education. At the end of the paper, he credited the experience in my office as the time when he began "to get his head together." With unsurpassed eloquence, he wrote, "When I walked out of that office, every tree for miles around was marked with self-respect." Having found a focus in the will of God, he regained his self-respect and discovered his potential for wholeness.

A Theory of Persons

Jesus' working theory is that a person has intrinsic worth, individualized differences, and interdependent functions. Human beings have value, not because of their original goodness, but because their potential for maturity testifies to God's creative purpose.

Infinite variation among persons does not dilute human potential. Jesus taught the principle of individual differences and responded to persons at their level of need. He did not impose arbitrary standards that violated an individual's integrity or establish a stereotype for discipleship that left no room for special talent. Consistent with God's design for complementary differences in his creation, each person has the capacity for maturity that will be uniquely expressed.

Jesus' principles of personhood focus in the unity of human nature. Body, mind, and soul are married in sickness and in health. Spiritual wholeness cannot be isolated from physical health or psychological maturity. To fulfill this principle, Jesus always responded to the totality of persons, never to physical, psychological, or spiritual pieces. By his own words and acts, he declared that persons are valuable beyond words, unique beyond description, and unified beyond the parts.

Chapter Seven

DYNAMICS OF WHOLENESS

ONE CANNOT remain neutral in a study of the personality of Jesus. Albert Schweitzer started out with a scholarly treatise on Jesus' mental health and finished with a missionary career of more than fifty years in Africa. Less dramatically, but with equal significance, we have seen Jesus as a real and complete man who shows us the potential of our human nature. Through the temptation, we have been stretched to develop the disciplines of prayer, scriptural knowledge, and obedience that led him to maturity. Jesus has become a "significant other" for us. It should be no surprise, then, to learn that our study has led to the "dynamics of wholeness" that Jesus outlined by his command and promise.

WHOLENESS IS A COMMAND

Pressed to give the greatest commandment, Jesus replied:

"Thou shalt love the Lord thy God with all thy heart, and
with all thy soul and with all thy mind." This is the first
and great commandment. And there is a second like it:
"Thou shalt love thy neighbor as thyself." The whole of the
Law and the Prophets depends upon these two commandments (Matt. 22:37–40).

In a radical departure from traditional theology, Jesus said
that the quality of a man's spiritual life was a matter of
relationships, not *rituals.* Two interacting and intersecting
dimensions of relationship were defined: one was a person's
vertical relationship to God; the other was his or her *horizontal* relationship with other persons.

Jesus' growth as a person reveals the factors that determine the quality of these relationships. He was linked to
God by his *self-consciousness* (awareness of being) and to
other persons by his *self-concept* (awareness of value).

Self-consciousness is the feature that distinguishes human
beings from all other forms of life. In Genesis, a person is
defined as a "living soul" (Gen. 2:7) created "in the image
of God" (Gen. 1:27). A human being's heritage included an
awareness of his or her separate identity—different from
God, other humans, animals, and the rest of creation. Persons
alone could commune with God in a relationship of respect
for each other's identity, authority, and responsibility. Only
when they chose to enter a contest of consciousness was the
beauty of the relationship broken. Not content to discover
the full meaning of human self-consciousness in the will (or
consciousness) of God, the man and woman sought their own
sovereignty. The rebellion failed, and they became outcasts
from the presence of God and fugitives from themselves.

One purpose of the Incarnation was to show men and
women what Adam missed. In the temptation, Jesus re-
entered the contest of consciousness. Where Adam sinned,
Christ obeyed. As we have seen, he came through temptation
with his self-consciousness totally merged with the consciousness of God. From then on, under daily test in different

situations, the will of God was the controlling center for Jesus' life and work. He reestablished God's authority over human life with the assurance that "the Son can do nothing of his own accord" (John 5:19). By his obedience, communion between God and humanity was restored in a single identity: "I am in the Father and the Father is in me" (John 14:10). "The man who has seen me has seen the Father" (John 14:9).

Everything Jesus did was aimed at helping people find the meaning of a restored relationship with God. He, the Word made flesh, was the example of a God-conscious man in action with the intention of transferring his relationship with the Father to his followers through himself. To achieve that end, he reminded them, "You must hold on to your faith in God and to your faith in me" (John 14:1). This opened the possibility of a spiritual quantum leap to the goal: "You are to be perfect, like your Heavenly Father" (Matt. 5:48). Futility and frustration would have followed this command except that Jesus also intervened with the prayer to his Father "that they may be one, as we are one—I in them and you in me" (John 17:22–23). His command for perfection must always be read in the context of his prayer for unity. As Jesus had fused his self-consciousness with the consciousness of God, in turn he asked that his disciples lose their self-consciousness in the identification with his mind and will. Time has not changed the prerequisite for spritual maturity.

Bruce Larson, a champion for the rediscovery of relational theology, writes, "Relational theology simply emphasizes the central fact of all the Bible: man's relationship to God on his terms, a relationship between Forgiver and forgiven, between Lover and loved." [1]

Human relationships develop on a dimension complementary to the relationship with God. Jesus also commanded, *"Thou shalt love thy neighbor as thyself"* (Matt. 19:19).

Secondary to the first commandment only in sequence, it is the practical outworking of a person's relationship to God. You must love God *before* you can love yourself; and you must love yourself *before* you can love someone else. The fulcrum is your *self-concept*—an awareness of identity and the value one puts on his or her personhood.

Insight and integration are the key factors in developing the self-concept. If individuals lack knowledge of their motives or have no focus for their drives, they will erect defenses to protect themselves from exposure in these areas; yet because personality cannot be divided into parts, they cannot be selectively defensive. Threats of exposure will be generalized until a defensive attitude characterizes their total life response. In the daily rubs with people, neutral cues and nonrelated symbols get charged with negative meaning so that the whole environment becomes a threat. Reacting protectively, the threatened party will begin to exhibit extreme symptoms of attack or escape that are out of proportion to the stimulus.

A man came to my office to inform me that he was Jesus Christ. By deciphering his name on the numbers of the cabala, he had concluded that he was Perfection. Thus, all authority over heaven and earth was in his hand. Pointing out the window to a break of blue in the clouds, he observed, "Did you notice the gray sky this morning? I was depressed. But now that I'm feeling better, my sun is beginning to shine." Rambling on, he spoke of a stoplight that turned green just as he arrived at the intersection and news reports that he controlled. "If I were not Perfect Love," he said, "I would destroy you with a snap of my fingers." Later on a psychiatrist who saw him reported that he would not become violent even though he had repeated a death threat against me. Frankly, I rested uneasily in the assurance of the psychiatrist. After all, it was my life, not his, that was threatened.

Healthy human relationships cannot be nourished in a climate of threat. Individuals are attacked or rejected when they need to be accepted. Rather than responding person-to-person, every cue of spoken word, facial expression, or body movement is checked as a threat to a tender ego. A vicious circle soon develops. Each new threat demands more formidable defenses, and in turn, the defenses make the person more sensitive to threat. Around and around, the greater the defenses, the less individuals know about themselves, and the more they reject people in order to avoid being exposed or hurt. Pulling their devalued self-concept into a protective womb, they stop growing toward their potential as open, creative, and whole persons—certainly they cannot love their neighbor because they do not love themselves. A neurotic is a person who makes other people sick.

Jesus foresaw the possibility that persons could develop a concept of self-love that permitted them to accept others because they accepted themselves. Exaggerated defenses would not have to be erected to compensate for lack of insight, nor would false reasons be invented for unintegrated behavior. Other individuals could be accepted as valuable, unique, and total personalities. In such relationships, people would grow together rather than shrink and pull apart.

C. S. Lewis gave this principle eternal dimensions in *The Great Divorce*.[2] Hell is a condition of human relationships with "self" at the center so that people shrink and flee from themselves and each other. Christ at the center of heaven makes the difference between the two worlds. As persons lose themselves in the image of Christ, they grow together and move toward the center.

Personally, Jesus lifted the commandment "Thou shalt love thy neighbor as thyself" to the highest level of human relationships. From his teaching, we infer three levels of love. At the minimal level, Jesus asked that his disciples have a love for their neighbors on a par with their own self-love. When queried, "Who is my 'neighbor?'" (Luke 10:29), Jesus raised self-love another notch to the level of loving even the heathen and enemies. Then, rather than preaching about the third level of human love, he acted it out by sacrificing his life for friends and enemies, heathens and sinners. Personal experience fills his provocative statement with meaning: "There is no greater love than this—that a man should lay down his life for his friends" (John 15:13). Later on, Paul the apostle staggered under the impact of the truth: *"While we were sinners . . .* Christ died for us" (Rom. 5:8). Self-sacrifice is the highest level of human love.

Two principles of interpersonal relationships follow from the commandment, "Thou shalt love thy neighbor as thyself." One is that an individual's degree of personal insight determines his or her ability to accept persons; the other is that the degree of personal integration determines the value that he or she places on other people.

When these principles permeate the person who is "in Christ," he or she is a "new creation," but the focus does not remain on spiritual development toward isolated perfectionism. Consistent with Christ's example and teaching, the "new creation" is worked out in relationships with God and man. Relational theology draws the bottom line for the new creation in Christ as "someone who can affirm others in the same way that Christ has affirmed us." [3]

Through the centuries, the priority and the sequence of loving God and loving others has been debated. Although Jesus first commanded us to love God, the two dimensions are so inseparable that he could reverse the process without violating the principle:

> . . . If, while you are offering your gift at the altar, you should remember that your brother has something against

you, you must leave your gift there before the altar and go away. Make your peace with your brother first, then come and offer your gift (Matt. 5:23–24).

John caught the same spirit when he made the love of one's brother the test of one's love of God:

> Here we have a clear indication as to who are the children of God and who are the children of the devil. The man who does not lead a good life is no son of God, nor is the man who fails to love his brother. . . . But as for the well-to-do man who sees his brother in want but shuts his eyes—and his heart—how could anyone believe that the love of God lives in him? (1 John 3:10, 17).

In the dynamics of wholeness, the love of God, the love of self, and the love of a brother are inextricably entwined. Whether by revivalists or reformers, evangelists or educators, prayers or picketers, any attempt to break the gospel into pieces is to distort the model of wholeness given us by Jesus Christ.

Promises of Wholeness

Jesus' call for wholeness was matched by his promises for the whole person. At one time or another during his ministry, he offered his followers an abundant *life,* overflowing *joy,* unprecedented *freedom,* and inner *peace.* At first, the list sounds like the utopian promises of an idealistic reformer or the campaign pledge of a political hopeful. Nothing in Jesus' life smacked of this kind of "promise them anything" philosophy. He only promised what he had experienced. Because of the quality of his own life, the promises of life, joy, freedom, and peace are realistic benefits of Christian maturity.

Fullness of Life. Jesus said, "I came to bring them life, and far more life than before" (John 10:10). Is it one thing to live and another thing to live to the fullest? Theologically, through the redemptive work of Jesus, Christians are persons who have passed from death to life. It is difficult to think of Christians who are just barely alive, but it must be so. Jesus seemed to recognize degrees in the quality of living when he promised life and then added "far more life than before."

Winston Churchill is one of my heroes. His unforgettable character was fashioned out of oratory, painting, and diplomacy as well as out of failure and booze. But the source of his unforgettable greatness was tapped by Norman Cousins in a memorial tribute as he recalled the pudgy figure with the black coat, black bowler, and equally black cigar striding over the rubble each morning after a Nazi air attack and reminding his people, "We have just begun to fight." Writing in *Saturday Review,* Cousins said that Churchill's greatness was his ability to "speak to the strength inside of people and to cause that strength then to come into being." He said because of Winston Churchill, millions of people discovered what it means to come fully alive:

> They knew that they faced total danger, but he helped them find their capacity for total response. They also learned that it was far less painful to pit the whole of themselves against the monstrous force than it was to sit on the sidelines half alive.[4]

Creativity is a quality of abundant living. We humans must have new experiences as a part of our need for self-actualization. Immaturity limits the range of these experiences because of the demands of baser needs, threats against ego defenses, and the wasted energies of internal conflict. After Jesus resolved these issues in his own life, he lived on the growing edge of spiritual meaning, social relationships, and human service. His creativity confounded the people who could not understand him, his friends, or his energetic action.

Like other creative people, he had the perspective to "break out" of the vicious cycles in which most of us are trapped. In contemporary terms, Jesus was a "big picture" man. His analysis of specific human and social problems was in the context of the larger setting and the long-term implications. For those with tunnel vision or nearsightedness, the creativity of Jesus was confounding and even threatening; yet for those who learned from him, creativity was promised as a part of the new life.

Concentration is another asset of the life that Jesus promises. Studies of gifted individuals show unusual ability to give full attention to the task or experience in which they find themselves. They do not half-work and half-play or look over the shoulder of the person to whom they are talking. By being "fully present" when others are mentally or emotionally absent, they perform tasks and solve problems that astound observers. The Pharisees could not understand a religious leader who enjoyed himself at parties or a miracle worker who paid attention to children. Yet this is what Jesus meant when he promised us "far more life than before"—to be pushing out the boundaries of human experience and giving full attention to the opportunity at hand. No wonder that Paul wrote, "The whole creation is on tiptoe to see the wonderful sight of the sons of God coming into their own" (Rom. 8:19).

Freedom. "You will know the truth and the truth will set you free" (John 8:32) is another benefit of Jesus' "far more life than before" compact. Opposing the advocates of freedom without substance, this promise makes the discipline of truth the liberator of men.

Student protest in the late 1960s and early 1970s exposed the fallacy of freedom without substance. Acting out of frustration with a society built on the bomb, the tube, and the computer, students tried to bring down the system without knowing why or considering the options. During the days of protest, one observer remarked that the scholarly Marx writing *Das Kapital* in his study was far more dangerous than Jerry Rubin on the streets shouting "Do it." Without substance to support their cry for freedom, the rebels either joined the system or disappeared as charred characters of the "burnt-out generation." To assume that undisciplined freedom precedes and produces truth cancels out both sides of the equation.[5]

Liberation theology has the sequence right, but the source of truth is wrong. Developing a hybrid theology of Christian doctrine and Marxist philosophy presumes that syncretism will lead to freedom. Early advocates of liberation theology quickly revealed a political evangelism that played into the hands of revolutionaries and deceived theologically unsophisticated Christians who could not sort out the contradictions of truth. Like its predecessors in theological fads, liberation theology runs the danger of becoming just another footnote in contemporary religious history. The strands of truth that remain will be consistent with the radical truth of the Word of God.

Jesus used the authority of Scriptures as his source for truth. When he invoked this authority, as with the Samaritan woman and the Pharisees, his purpose was to show the inconsistency between their inner life and the standard of the Word of God. Truth must have this objectivity if a person is to be delivered from the slavery of his or her baser desires. Even though truth, like the insight it invokes, is painful, the result is the freedom to "live inside out"—a characteristic of Christian maturity which permits the exploration of the inner man and the search for higher values as a part of personal growth.

A preacher, in an exalted moment, struck the tone for the

freedom which Christ promised when he exclaimed, "To be redeemed is to be awakened by the sound of a thousand trumpets and find it bliss to be alive in such a dawn as this."

Joy. An elusive dream of humanity was fulfilled when Jesus gave the promise:

> I have loved you just as the Father has loved me. You must go on living in my love. If you keep my commandments you will live in my love just as I have kept my Father's commandments and live in his love. I have told you this so that you can share my joy, and that your happiness may be complete (John 15:9–11).

Love and joy are two different expressions of wholeness. The difference is that *love has a person as its object* and *joy is task-oriented.* A common error is to seek joy as an end rather than as a means. To be sure, it was a goal for Jesus, who "endured a cross and thought nothing of its shame because of the *joy* he knew would follow his suffering" (Heb. 12:2, italics mine). Jesus' promise to his disciples, however, referred to the present joy that he found living in full communion with his Father. His joy was a practical result of loving God with all his heart, soul, mind, and strength, but it was more than this. Jesus also was obedient to the will of the Father in fulfilling his mission. He found joy in his ongoing ministry as well as in anticipating his future status. Joy cannot be deferred any more than it can be sought. Persons who believe that they will find joy "if only" certain things come to pass will be forever waiting.

When C. S. Lewis searched for joy in mental images and physical sensations, he found that ". . . they were merely the mental track left by the passage of Joy—not the wave but the wave's imprint on the sand." [6]

Surprise awaited Lewis when his search for joy led him to Christ.

> But what, in conclusion, of Joy? . . . To tell you the truth,
> the subject has lost nearly all interest for me since I became
> a Christian. . . . When we are lost in the woods the sight of
> a signpost is a great matter. . . . But when we have found
> the road and are passing signposts every few miles, we shall
> not stop and stare. . . . "We would be at Jerusalem." [7]

As Lewis discovered, joy is not a fringe benefit of redemption; it is integral to the Christian's existence. Again,
Jesus is our model, for he made joy a quality of "being"
and "doing." He gave thanks in difficult circumstances, enjoyed social situations under criticism, used humor under
pressure, and sang a hymn on the eve of his crucifixion. It is
wrong to think, however, that Jesus was a Pollyanna. He
neither laughed when he should have cried nor sang when he
should have prayed. Joy was a quality of his life because
he put each moment and each task in the perspective of his
total mission. He knew who he was, why he was here, and
where he was going. To be about his Father's business was the
élan vital that baffled those who did not know him. An
overflowing source, this is the same joy that he promised to
men who were made whole.

Peace. As his last will and testament for the disciples,
Jesus left his peace. He said, "I leave behind with you—
peace; I give you my own peace and my gift is nothing like
the peace of this world" (John 14:27). Like a territorial line
of demarcation, Jesus drew the distinction between his peace
and the peace of the world. Perhaps he had in mind Jeremiah's prophecy that people would cry "Peace, peace; when
there is no peace" (Jer. 6:14, KJV). To this, he would later
add his own apocalyptic note about the false hopes for peace
in the world as he warned his disciples, "You will hear of
wars and rumors of wars" (Matt. 24:6).

Jesus may still have had war in mind when he described
his peace as "nothing like" the peace of this world. In those

rare moments when wars cease among nations, peace is kept
by a truce that is no stronger than the force behind it. War
can break out any time because hate and greed are not
eliminated by signed agreements. At best, the peace of the
world is tenuous on the surface and underridden with
anxiety.

A weekly news magazine that came to the house recently
featured our fears with the question on the cover, "Peace:
Can It Last?" At best, world leaders can subscribe to
"U-U optimism" for peace on earth. "U-U" means "unmiti-
gated uncertainty."

The peace that Jesus promised for the human spirit had
to be different. An armed truce or a paper agreement is not
enough; full resolution must be found for the conflict. The
only alternative is the full surrender of self-consciousness to
the consciousness of Christ. With this trust agreement, the
war is over even though the terms of surrender must be
worked out over a lifetime. Paul triumphantly resolved the
war in his spirit this way when he shouted, "I thank God
there *is* a way out through Jesus Christ our Lord" (Rom.
7:25).

Peace is the promise of wholeness that Jesus reserved for
the last. He waited until he had shown the disciples its
meaning in the crucible of life. Then, with the confidence of
his own experience, he gave them the legacy of his peace.

Napoleon said, "Trust God but keep your powder dry,"
and a comic spoke of having the confidence of a Christian
holding four aces. Neither knew the meaning of the peace
of Christ. It is not conditioned by dry powder or four aces.
Peace is won, according to Thomas à Kempis in *The Imitation of Christ,* by four commitments:

> Be desirous, my son, to do the will of another
>   rather than thine own.
> Choose always to have less rather than more.

Seek always the lowest place and to be beneath
  every one.
Wish always and pray that the will of God may
  be wholly fulfilled in thee.[8]

To follow these steps is to find the inward peace that
Jesus bequeathed to us as his last will and testament. It is
regretful that the inheritance is often unclaimed.

THE CELEBRATION OF WHOLENESS

Wholeness has the dynamics of both commandment and
promise. The command is twofold: a *Christ-consciousness* in
every function of mind, body, soul, and strength; a *person-
consciousness* in every human relationship, from neighbors
to enemies. Activated by love, the commandment becomes
the expression of a Christian personality with the qualities
of wholeness that Jesus promised. *Life* takes on the full range
of new experience and the power of full attention; *freedom*
for the pursuit of higher human and spiritual values comes
with the insight of objective truth into the inner life; *joy*
makes the process of life as meaningful as its goal; and *peace*
is the assurance of internal integrity through total surrender
to the person of Jesus Christ.

Christian worship is a celebration of wholeness. During
Jimmy Carter's presidential campaign, Norman Mailer went
to Plains, Georgia, to find the person behind the political
phenomenon. Out of a sense of journalistic duty rather than
personal devotion, Mailer attended Sunday morning worship at Carter's home church. When he wrote his story for
the *New York Times Magazine,* his pen took wings and fire
as he remembered the experience: "The choir sang the
hymns and the congregation sang with them, the words full
of Christian exaltation, their sword of love quivering in the
air, that secret in the strength of Christianity where the steel
is smelted from the tears." [9]

Through a simple hymn, Christians had again won a skeptic with the spirit of their life, freedom, joy, and peace.

Wholeness, then, is the dynamic experience to which a study of the personality of Jesus calls us. Initially, his commandment may seem heavy and his promises distant, but when Christians celebrate life, wholeness becomes a possibility for every person.

Part Four

THE PRACTICE OF JESUS

"... the Son of Man has not come to be served but to serve, and to give his life to set many others free."

Matthew 20:28

Chapter Eight

HIS COUNSELING

JESUS REFINED his principles of personhood in the fire of human relationships. In most instances, the Gospels give just a capsule comment about his encounters with people. On two or three occasions, though, the record of the conversation is extended so that the principles can be seen in process. Among these occasions, Jesus' meeting with the Samaritan woman at the well stands out as a detailed account of interpersonal action. In fact, enough is known about the thoughts and feelings of the two participants to reconstruct the encounter as a case study in counseling. Moving into the conversation in depth, we will see that the meeting discloses the *skills of Jesus* as a counselor, a *process for Christians who counsel,* and sets *standards for counseling theory*—both secular and Christian.

The Samaritan Woman: A Case Study
John 4:1–42

Setting: In biblical times, Sychar was a way-station between Judea and Galilee. Jacob had dug a water hole at this strategic intersection in the wasteland that separated north from south. Throughout the course of history, Samaria had become a ghetto for Jews who had intermarried with heathen tribes. Only a chance meeting would bring a purebred Jew like Jesus into contact with a Samaritan half-breed, particularly a woman.

As unlikely as the situation was, physical necessity overcame cultural barriers. Jesus was tired and thirsty. He rested on the well but had no way to get a drink. Therefore, when the Samaritan woman appeared with her waterpots, supply and demand took charge. Jesus' request for a drink of water led to an in-depth human encounter.

Format: With the detail provided by Scripture, the words of Jesus and the Samaritan woman can be studied for the interaction of ideas and feelings that led to the woman's confession of Christ. All the limitations of knowledge and nuance are accepted. The single intention is to learn more about the consistency between Jesus' personality development and the practice of his ministry. Therefore, a case-study form for counseling is followed with interpretive comments, which are related to the previous study of Jesus —a real, complete, and mature man.

Statement:	*Interpretation:*
Jesus: "Please give me a drink."	Every social and religious taboo was broken by Jesus' request. He spoke to a woman, a Samaritan, and the town divorcee. Also he indicated a willingness to drink from a common cup.
	By deliberate action, Jesus put the priority of physical need and personal

Statement:	*Interpretation:*

Statement:

Interpretation:

worth over social, sexual, and religious taboos.

Woman: "How can you, a Jew, ask for a drink from me, a woman of Samaria?"

The woman might have silently given the stranger a drink or bluntly said no to an enemy. Instead, she returned a feisty challenge to Jesus. Perhaps it was the hint of irony in her retort— a form of humor which requires intellectual perception and the capability of subdued rage. Or perhaps her response carried an early indicator of her need through the implied question, What do you really want? Later information supports the fact that she would suspect the motives of any man.

Jesus: "If you knew what God can give, and if you knew who it is that said to you, 'Give me a drink,' I think you would have asked him, and he would have given you living water!"

Somehow, by inflection, facial expression, or body language, the Samaritan woman had shown her need. Jesus responded by introducing himself and his ability to satisfy her deeper thirst. The analogy of the water kept the tie between the physical and spiritual aspects of the conversation.

At the same time, Jesus gave her a "readiness test" to see how desperate she was and how deep she was willing to go in a probe of her inner life. Her curiosity keeps the question open. Although her words still have an edge of sarcasm, the feelings are now mixed between desperation and hope.

Woman: "Sir, you have nothing to draw water with and this well is deep—where can you get your living water? Are you a greater man than our ancestor, Jacob, who gave us this well, and drank here himself

Jesus had gained enough of her trust to permit her to seek the common historical ground that they shared with their forefather Jacob.

Further evidence of her native intelligence is revealed by her precise

130

Statement:	Interpretation:

with his family, and his cattle?"

response to the content of Jesus' statement in the form of two questions of her own: "How can you satisfy my need?" and "Who are you to make this claim?" Jesus was leading gently, and she was urging him on.

Jesus: "Everyone who drinks this water will be thirsty again. But whoever drinks the water I will give him will never be thirsty again. For my gift will become a spring in the man himself, welling up into eternal life."

Pressing the analogy, Jesus crossed the boundary between the woman's physical and spiritual needs. He defined living water as eternally thirst-quenching and life-giving.

In response to her question, Jesus identified himself as the giver of living water, but the source is in the person. Two critical insights into spiritual development have been introduced: the person of Jesus and the individual's inner life.

Woman: "Sir, give me this water, so that I may stop being thirsty —and not have to come here to draw water any more!"

Skeptical questions and initial sarcasm had changed to "Sir"—the woman's recognition that she was in the presence of authority. Although she could not yet make the full transition from physical to spiritual water, she did confess the dreariness of her existence. More importantly, she expressed her willingness to trust the stranger.

Jesus: "Go and call your husband and then come back here."

To this point, the woman had been asking practical questions while Jesus was using spiritual metaphors. Now Jesus took the initiative with an incisive command that would determine whether or not the woman was really willing to face her need.

Jesus was not "shooting in the dark"

Statement: *Interpretation:*

with these instructions. Women with
the reputation of the Samaritan were
marked by dress and demeanor in the
Mideastern culture of the first century.

From every indication, the woman
was ready for him to move into the
center of her need. If Jesus' second
sentence had been, "Go, call your
husband," the conversation would
have ended abruptly. His sense of
timing, however, caused him to wait
until she had enough trust in him to
confess her need.

Woman: "I haven't got a husband!"

As might be expected, she sidestepped
the stab of truth. Despite her divorces
and a common-law husband, practice
had taught her how to parry questions and insults when she was threatened. What she didn't know was that
her defensive reaction also revealed
tinges of guilt.

Jesus: "You are quite right in saying, 'I haven't got a hus-band,' for you have had five husbands and the man you have now is not your hus-band at all. Yes, you spoke the simple truth when you said that."

Did Jesus exercise divine omniscience
in this instance? If he did, it repre-
sents one of the rare moments in the
Scriptures when he summoned this
power in personal conversation. More
likely, the reputation of the woman
was well known so that Jesus' sensitivity made it possible to draw con-
nections between the stories he had
heard and the woman he met.

In either case, it is now Jesus' turn
for a bit of irony as he says, "You
spoke the simple truth when you said
that!" By suggesting that she was de-
viously honest, he was showing her
the image in a "looking-glass self"

132

Statement:	*Interpretation:*
	that she needed to see for self-objectification. All the excuses about heredity and cultural determinism fell away before the hard fact that she was personally responsible for her immorality and her dishonesty.
Woman: "I can see that you are a prophet! Now our ancestors worshiped on this hillside, but you Jews say that Jerusalem is the place where men ought to worship—"	Jesus knew too much! A hidden assumption is that he might have gone on to expose other dark areas of her life. Guilt rushes in and builds a defense. With the humor of the ludicrous, her nervous answer might be paraphrased, "Oh, I see that you are a prophet—let's talk about prophecy." Anything was preferable to further exposure. Her high level of intelligence almost comes to her rescue. If she can get Jesus entangled in a Jewish-Samaritan controversy, it will take the emotional pressure off her personal life. By now, however, even her defense is a sign of hope because insight is always painful and religious issues are always safer than scrutiny. Did Jesus move too fast? Probably not. His incisive probe opened up a "zoo of lusts" in her subconscious self, but she did not reject him. Rather, she "came up for air" by temporarily substituting an intellectual issue for her emotional conflict.
Jesus: "Believe me, the time is coming when worshiping the Father will not be a matter of 'on this hill-	Sensitive to her pain, Jesus gives her relief. Rather than forcing her deeper into her inner life, he accepts the controversial question and uses it as an opportunity to state a universal truth.

Statement:

side' or 'in Jerusalem.' Nowadays you are worshiping with your eyes shut. We Jews are worshiping with our eyes open, for the salvation of mankind is to come from our race. Yet the time is coming, yes, and has already come, when true worshipers will worship the Father in spirit and in reality. Indeed, the Father looks for men who will worship him like that. God is Spirit, and those who worship him can only worship in spirit and in reality."

Woman: "Of course I know that Messiah is coming, you know, the one who is called Christ. When he comes he will make everything plain to us."

Jesus: "*I am Christ, speaking to you now.*"

Interpretation:

Perhaps we dismissed the genuineness of the woman's concern over the issue of worship too quickly. If she followed Jesus, a Jew, sooner or later she would have to solve the question of where she worshiped. How often religious controversies are obstacles in the way of personal salvation!

As he continued his response to her dilemma, Jesus took the woman back into herself again by emphasizing that the inner life is the point of communication with God. Then, with a remarkable show of counseling skill, Jesus took an irreconcilable conflict and used it as a promise of reconciliation. He paid the woman a supreme compliment by assuming that she could draw the parallel between his resolution of the ancient controversy and the war that raged in her own soul.

Jesus' compliment is rewarded by the woman's response. She awaits Messiah as the person to bring her conflicts to an end and to make her life whole. Intellectually, she has shown the latent ability to cope with some of the most complex theological issues. This is not enough. She also needs a Messiah with the power to transform her life; so, with a desperate thrust, she put out her straw of hope that this stranger might be the Christ.

Jesus revealed his divine nature more openly to this Samaritan woman than he did to his own disciples. Her total

134

Statement: *Interpretation:*

honesty and profound insight had
brought her to the edge of readiness
for redemption. In other situations,
Jesus had to conceal his identity in
order to avoid exploitation by persons with mixed motives or partial
insight. In this case, he could afford
to take the full risk of revelation because the woman was so open and
perceptive. Is it possible that Jesus had
this experience in mind when he told
the chief priests and elders that "tax
collectors and prostitutes are going
into the kingdom of God in front of
you (Matt. 21:31)?

Jesus counseled to a decision. With
the revelation of his person, the conversation became a confrontation
which left the woman with a decision.
In accord with his basic respect for
persons, Jesus did not force the
woman to a choice. Yet sooner or
later she would have to decide whether to reject her new-found insight
and sink into deeper sin or risk her
life with a stranger who claimed to be
the Messiah in order that she might
be made whole.

Conclusion: At that moment, the disciples returned to the
scene. The Gospel writer John reported that they were
shocked by Jesus' violation of the rabbinical law against
teaching the Scriptures privately to a woman. Caught in the
middle, the Samaritan woman left her waterpots, ran to the
town, and announced to all who would listen, "Come out and
see the man who told me everything I've ever done! Can
this be 'Christ'?" Now we have the evidence that Jesus' incisive knowledge of her past had brought into the light the

total view of her sin and need. Even though her announcement of Christ was framed as a question, it was her public confession of faith. For a woman who had lost credibility in her community, she gave a daring and undeniable testimony!

Nothing more is known about this woman except that the Samaritans of Sychar rushed out to Jesus, took him in as their guest, and many put their trust in him during the two-day visit. Striking significance is found in the conclusion of the townspeople who believed on Jesus. They came back to the woman and said:

> We don't believe any longer now because of what you said. We have heard him with our own ears. We know now that this must be the man who will save the world!

Even though her fellow citizens could not quite forgive the Hester Prynne of their village, neither could they help paying her the backhanded compliment of acknowledging her belief in Christ and awkwardly thanking her for introducing him to them.

JESUS, THE COUNSELOR

Ease and spontaneity characterized Jesus' conversation with the woman at the well, but behind the scenes there is evidence of a conscious design. Using the principles of personhood that he had learned from his own experience, Jesus led the woman through a series of steps toward psychological and spiritual wholeness. Undoubtedly, his timing and sequence would vary from individual to individual, but the general principles of Jesus' interaction with persons would remain the same.

First, Jesus accepted the woman as a person. In addition to violating all the taboos that stood between him and the woman, Jesus paid full respect to her individuality. Her veiled sarcasm as well as her honest questions were equally

accepted without judgment. As part of his acceptance, Jesus
let the woman establish the initial level at which their conversation took place. In this way, he let her know that she
was a unique and worthwhile person with the potential for
growth and wholeness.

Second, Jesus let her confess her personal need. Early condemnation, either by look or word, would have been the
expected response of a rabbi to a scarlet woman. In fact, the
woman's first question to Jesus intimated that she doubted
his real motive in asking for a drink. Jesus, however, let her
choose her own timing to reveal the depth of her need. When
the woman did, she threw herself wide open to full exposure
and let it be known that she wanted her life changed. An
unusual case, the Samaritan woman had lost almost all her
defenses when she lost her reputation. Psychologically, she
had nothing to unlearn before she was ready to learn!

Third, Jesus provided insight into the woman's inner life.
Most counselors would oppose Jesus' sharp probe into the
woman's sordid past. If she could not have faced this level
of truth, Jesus' statement would have been premature and
even damaging. The test of the wisdom, however, is the
outcome. At first it was too much for the woman to absorb,
but later she used Jesus' statement in public testimony to
support her announcement that she had met the Christ. It is
reasonable, then, to assume that Jesus used the trauma of
exposing her inner life in order to break the vicious cycle
that had led her in and out of marriage and divorce. His
probe uncovered a subconscious pool of guilt, but, contrary
to those who contend that guilt is bad, Jesus actually encouraged the expression of guilt as the natural result of
insight.

Guilt has been described as the recognition of the dis-
crepancy between the "ought" and the "is" in a person's life.
If the difference is so great that there seems to be no recovery,
neurotic defenses are erected to bridge the gap. By his

presence, Jesus showed the "ought" of God's standard and the "is" of the woman's life as a gap that she had unsuccessfully tried to rationalize or fill in with the senses. Each new sin widened the gap and perpetuated a compulsive cycle of failure and escape through sex. Therefore, Jesus knew that the way to wholeness for the woman had to include the pain of deep insight and the agony of extensive guilt.

Fourth, Jesus promised the woman release from her guilt. Even before Jesus exposed the woman's past life, he made it clear that he could quench her compulsive thirst. There was more to this promise than just the theological hope of redemption. Healing also has a psychological dimension as a step toward wholeness. To gain insight, a person needs to be related to an objective source—another person—who can absorb hostility without retaliation and point out the direction for growth without condescension. Complete and mutual trust is required of both parties, with one member being a "model" of maturity.

Jesus was this kind of person. In contemporary language, he was a "significant other." His maturity invited needy people to trust him at the same time that he threatened those who were deceitfully self-assured. Psychologically, he was whole but not out of reach. Spiritually, he was holy but not "holier than thou." Jesus helped the Samaritan woman grow even before she realized who he was.

Fifth, Jesus offered himself to the woman as the focus for personal wholeness. Her need was confessed, her past life was before her eyes, and her guilt was out in the open—now the woman needed to bring these forces into the cataclysm of conversion. Simply put, she needed the single center of a new affection to transform her life. Translated into the psychological criteria for maturity, the woman still lacked a unifying philosophy of life.

Some measure of maturity might have been won if she had given herself to a new idea, a lofty cause, or a self-denying goal, but her guilt would remain, and she would miss the dynamic of identification with a person. That is why the concept of Christian maturity is fulfilled in the personality of Jesus. No other person can claim absolute integrity in all dimensions of life. In his growth and maturity, we can identify with the process in which he learned to understand, discipline, and finally give himself for others. Our case study closes with the evidence that the Samaritan woman discovered the meaning of maturity in the Person of Jesus, of whom she asked, "Can this be 'Christ'?"

CRITERIA FOR CHRISTIAN COUNSELING

Jesus' role as a counselor bears directly on the contemporary interest in counseling—both secular and Christian. Almost daily, another technique hits the market adding to the field that is already flooded; yet if these new therapies are analyzed in depth, they are most often semantical nuances based on existing personality theory or counseling methods. To get behind the fluff of scholarly egos and the puff of sensational salesmanship, some criteria for critical discrimination need to be set.

Our case study of Jesus and the Samaritan woman gives us three standards for judging old and new counseling theories. First and foremost is the need for the *personal maturity of the counselor.* By various lateral moves in theory and practice, secular counseling has tried to side-step the personality of the counselor in the healing process. Presumably, with adequate professional preparation and techniques, a person can be effective in therapy with minimum regard for maturity and integrity outside the counseling office. Some safeguards have been erected by state-controlled licensing, a professional code of ethics, and the optional practice of counselors undergoing therapy themselves. Still, there is no guarantee that a credentialed counselor is a physician who has healed himself or a person who is moving toward maturity. Too often, the practitioner reinforces the stereotype of a counselor as a person who has chosen the field as an escape from his own problems. Ironically, during a break in writing this section, I was in a barber shop and picked up a national magazine that featured an "inside look" at the life of a prominent authority in psychiatry and counseling theory. Behind the mind and the reputation were tragic failures in marriage and human relationships.

Jesus set a different standard with the tested quality of his personal life. Like any skilled counselor, he was "empathetic" with the woman at the well because he was subject to the same human needs that motivated her. Here the separation begins. Jesus also had "insight" that permitted him to understand and channel his full humanity within the larger perspective of his mission in the will of God. Then, by the discipline of obedience, he was a man who was maintaining his integrity and moving toward new levels of maturity under test. Thus, Jesus stands apart from empathetic and insightful counselors who stop short of integrity or maturity. When he brought his personal experience of empathy, insight, and maturity to his meeting with the Samaritan woman, he raised an expectation for counselors that Christians must seek and secularists cannot ignore.

The second standard is the *counselee's need for redemptive resources*. At the root of the standard is the question of the inherent good or evil of the human personality. With only the rarest exceptions, secular counselors begin with the assumption that a person is capable of self-healing. Accordingly, a counselor's task is to identify, support, and direct the inner resources, which are naturally predisposed toward emotional health. A thin but definitive line is drawn for counseling when original sin is introduced into personality theory. Jesus paid full respect to the Samaritan woman as a person created in the image of God—unique, valuable, and free. Calling out these resources, he led her beyond her sensuality to uncommon honesty and unexpected hope. Here, her resources began to dwindle. Through rigorous self-discipline, she might have been able to turn her life around and resist the old habits that drove her. Like an old hate, however, the hatchet could have been buried, but the handle would always be close to the surface. Even though she might achieve a measure of integrity through self-discipline, her past would haunt her, and her future would be filled with the fear of relapse.

The Samaritan woman needed to be forgiven of the past and freed for the future. Within herself, she lacked the power to make the final leap to healing. In that conclusive moment, her human nature was an obstacle rather than a resource. Only God in the Person of Jesus Christ could intervene; so, to bring her from hope to healing, Jesus took the risk of an exclusive revelation of his deity by announcing, "I am Christ speaking to you now."

Counseling divides between a secular and Christian context at the point of redemptive resources. Secularists presuppose a continuous line of self-healing that leads to wholeness. Christians put full confidence in the resources of a person who is created in the image of God but stop short of wholeness without the intervention of divine resources for forgiveness and the power to lead a new life. Any counseling theory or technique that posits spiritual maturity without spiritual reconciliation is weighed and found wanting according to the example set by Jesus with the woman at the well.

The third standard for the critical appraisal of counseling techniques is the *counselor's need for professional preparation*. While certified counselors jealously guard their domain in the secular realm, the Christian community is inundated by laymen's counseling movements. Assuming a maximum of spiritual experience and biblical knowledge with a minimum of professional preparation, the implication is that every believer can be a counselor. Such thinking is an arrogant contradiction of Jesus' model. Not only did he have a maturity nurtured in discipline and a theory of personality fashioned from experience, but he had a sound method of counseling, which continues to be confirmed by research and practice today. To assume, therefore, that Christian experience and biblical knowledge qualify a person with limited professional preparation to be a counselor is a fallacy. If truth in labeling is applied to many of the counseling techniques recommended for Christians today, they would be more appropriately named "spiritual precounseling," "sympathetic evangelism," or "redemptive listening." To meet the standard set by Jesus, Christian counseling must be a discipline defined by specific professional as well as personal requirements.

On balance, secular counseling puts the weight on the professional preparation of the counselor and on the self-healing resources of the counselee. Christian counseling rights the scale with expectations for personal integrity, biblical knowledge, and a realistic view of the nature of men and women. In the hands of opportunists, however, Christian counseling can fall prey to an easy professionalism that lacks the humility needed by any therapist who deals with the complexity and depth of the human personality. Whether the counseling is Christian or secular, Jesus has set standards for critical appraisal: Is *personal maturity* expected of a counselor? Are *redemptive resources* available to the counselee? Is *professional preparation* required of the counselor?

Having stressed the qualifications, skills, and standards of Jesus the counselor, we cannot forget the dynamic of his Spirit when he met the woman at the well. Whether we are professional counselors or person-centered laymen, his Spirit in human relationships is our example. If we are to continue his work with people, we too must have the *love of God* to accept them, the *authority of truth* to challenge them, the

142

example of maturity to give them hope, and the *experience of redemption* to introduce them to Jesus Christ. Otherwise, we will seldom get beyond asking needy people for a drink of water.

Chapter Nine

HIS TEACHING

JESUS WAS called Rabbi—master teacher—by both friends
and enemies. He earned the title, not by formal education,
but by the clarity and authority of his teaching. Unlike many
rabbis, Jesus added the vigor of his spirit and the reality of
his experience to make learning come to life; yet he did not
teach by whimsy. He led his disciples through a planned
process that resulted in intellectual as well as spiritual insight. Jesus, the teacher, is a worthy subject for study in an
age dominated by education as an agent for social change
and personal growth.

A MOBILE CLASSROOM

One example of Jesus' teaching is his walk to Emmaus with
Cleopas and a friend on the day of the resurrection. Seven

miles of dusty road separated the two cities. Assuming that a "conversational mile" on a hot day takes at least twenty minutes to walk, the seminar must have lasted two or more hours. The two men were heading home after three days of waiting for their Master to return from the dead. As disciples of Jesus, they were absorbed in thoughtful conversation about the events of the past few days. Their surprise companion and visiting lecturer was Jesus himself. At first, they did not know him; so with the advantage of anonymity, Jesus led them through a full cycle of effective learning. In case-study form, this educational experience adapts itself to a running commentary on the dialogue between the teacher and his students; as written in Luke 24:13–35.

THE CASE STUDY

Setting:
Dialogue:

Interpretation:

"Then on the same day we find two of them going off to Emmaus, a village about seven miles from Jerusalem. As they went they were deep in conversation about everything that had happened.

Three conditions for effective learning are present. *First,* the men were engrossed in open, personal communication, not in an artificial classroom setting where forced feeding takes place. *Second,* they were totally involved in the dialogue as they *walked, talked,* and *reasoned* together. *Third,* Cleopas and his friend were frustrated because their knowledge was uncertain, and their patience was exhausted. In effect, they were asking the primary question, How can I know what I think until I feel what I do?

Setting:
Dialogue:

Interpretation:

"While they were absorbed in their serious talk and discussion, Jesus himself approached and walked along with them, but something prevented them from recognizing him.

Good teaching begins with good listening. Rather than choosing a dramatic confrontation, Jesus just fell into step as an interested partner in an animated conversation.

Jesus: "What is all this discussion that you are having on your walk?"

Jesus immediately perceived that the motivation for learning was present, but wanting to build in them a reasoned faith, he remained anonymous. With the stroke of a master teacher, he asked two interrelated questions: "What are you talking about?" and "Why are you feeling so sad?" In so doing, he asked to share in their feelings as well as in the substance of their conversation.

"They stopped, their faces drawn with misery."

Not unexpectedly, a teacher who begins with questions at the point of the students' needs wins full attention.

Cleopas: "You must be the only stranger in Jerusalem who hasn't heard all the things that have happened there recently!"

Cleopas' response to Jesus' leading question about the facts was one of surprise and mild skepticism. It was as if he said, "Where in the world have you been?" Also, he was not yet ready to let this

Setting: *Dialogue:*	*Interpretation:*
	stranger know his feelings until he knew his intentions.
Jesus: "What things?"	Jesus still refused to let the focus of attention shift to himself. Rather, with tongue in cheek, he pleaded innocent by asking another open-ended question. In Socratic style, he led the learners along in order to stimulate self-learning and develop a climate of trust in which they would share their feelings with him. No teaching device is more effective for tapping the growth potential of students than questions that cannot be answered yes or no.
Cleopas or Friend: "Oh, all about Jesus from Nazareth. There was a man—a prophet strong in what he did and what he said, in God's eyes as well as the people's. Haven't you heard how our chief priests and rulers handed him over for execution, and had him crucified? But we were hoping he was the one who was to come and set Israel free. . . ."	An extended response was the reward for Jesus' patience. The men indicated that they had some important facts in hand which became more objective as they related them to Jesus, but behind the substance of their knowledge were some overpowering feelings of doubt. Twice in this response, they said, "Yes, but . . . ," which actually meant no. *First,* after citing the reputation of Jesus as a prophet and teacher, they said, "*But we were hoping he was the one who was to come and set Israel free . . .*"

Setting:
Dialogue:

Interpretation:

"Yes, and as if that were not enough, it's getting on for three days since all this happened; and some of our womenfolk have disturbed us profoundly. For they went to the tomb at dawn, and then when they couldn't find his body they said that they had had a vision of angels who said that he was alive. Some of our people went straight off to the tomb and found things just as the women had described them—but they didn't see *him!*"

Often, facts which are accepted intellectually become a misconception when feelings are added. The men had the pieces of truth about Jesus as the Messiah, but they still wanted him to be a social liberator. *Second,* they told how the women had reported the Resurrection: *"But* they didn't see him!" Like Thomas, they were skeptics who had to be firsthand witnesses before they would believe.

Jesus, as a teacher, would be encouraged by their ambivalence because it meant that the men were now sharing with him the uncertainty of their knowledge and the depth of their despair.

Jesus: "Aren't you failing to understand, and slow to believe in all that the prophets have said? Was it not inevitable that Christ should suffer like that and so find his glory?"

Staying with questions, Jesus responded to their feelings by showing that he had feelings too. Again, his disciples had missed the point of his teaching about the purpose of his life and death. His first impulse was to rebuke them, but then he caught himself, turned to a substantive question, and patiently began all over again.

"Then, beginning with Moses and all

In a complete lecture, Jesus relied again on his discipline

148

Setting: Dialogue:	Interpretation:

the prophets, he explained to them everything in the scriptures that referred to himself."

in the Scriptures. Authoritatively, he traced each passage which addressed his identity and destiny. Then, inductively relating fact to fact, he drew a conclusion by synthesis that Jesus is the Christ and alive! Scriptural authority, a sense of history, and a logical conclusion were used to bolster the shaken faith of the disciples. Jesus' return to the objectivity of his scriptural authority proved again his principles that the truth has the power to set men free and that feelings cannot be separated from facts in human learning.

"They were by now approaching the village to which they were going. He gave the impression that he meant to go on further, but they stopped him with the words, 'Do stay with us. It is nearly evening and soon the day will be over.' So he went indoors to stay with them."

Typically, the formal lecture ended before the learning process was complete. Jesus had won the confidence and whetted the curiosity of the men even though they still did not know him. As an interim check on the progress of his teaching, Jesus pretended to be going beyond Emmaus. The invitation to dinner came, not just as an expression of Mideastern hospitality, but as the desire of the men to continue their conversation with a knowledgeable and encouraging companion.

Setting: *Dialogue:*	*Interpretation:*
"Then it happened! While he was sitting at the table with them he took the loaf, gave thanks, broke it and passed it to them. Their eyes opened wide and *they knew him!"*	Dinner with Jesus was more than an event; it was an experience. The men had been face-to-face with him for more than two hours; they had walked with him, answered his questions,⁻ and listened to his lecture. Yet they did not know him until he gave them the symbol of the broken bread.

A symbol is a problem-solving device that helps students pull the cognitive, affective, and volitional parts of learning into unified meaning. It is a Gestalt that produces the "Ah, ha" of a new insight. Using bread, the symbol of his death, and resetting the scene of the Last Supper, Jesus personalized the truth for them by joining his experience with theirs to arrive at conclusive proof.

Teaching that changes values and behavior almost invariably includes the personalization of the learning process through the mutual experience of the teacher and student.

Commonly, it is expected that the most effective learning requires a positive and satisfying stimulus. This is not necessarily true. Personal |

Setting: *Dialogue:*	*Interpretation:*
	tragedy may represent the deepest and most pervasive expressions of the human condition. Therefore, it also holds the potential for insightful learning. Rather than protecting students from the tragic, a master teacher uses the experience for positive results.
"But he vanished from their sight."	Jesus' part in the teaching-learning process was over. Sensitive to the situation, he knew when to leave in order to prevent knowledge over-kill or emotional overdependence.
Cleopas: "Weren't our hearts glowing while he was with us on the road, and when he made the scriptures so plain to us?"	The time had come for feedback and evaluation. When Cleopas knew the person, he also understood the process. Jesus' skill in teaching was now attested by the student's report that he "fired" their hopes and made the Scriptures plain. Master teachers are best remembered for their enthusiasm and simplicity. In the process, Jesus changed their fears to hope. Certainly the evaluation of a teacher's skill should be the ability to discover a student's level of motivation and raise it to a point of intensity where insight and integration become a possibility.

Setting: *Dialogue:*	*Interpretation:*
"And they got to their feet without delay and turned back to Jerusalem. There they found the eleven and their friends all together, full of the news—'The Lord is really risen—he has appeared to Simon now!'	The final test of learning is the student's ability to put knowledge into action. Cleopas and his friend turned around and went back to Jerusalem late at night. Once they were there, they told the disciples what they had learned and how they had learned it.
"Then they told the story of their walk, and how they recognized him when he broke the loaf."	For their authority, they used the symbol of the breaking of the bread. This was the common point of identification that everyone had experienced. Under questioning, Cleopas and his friend could communicate what they had learned with the force of personal knowledge and the proof of a common symbol. For them, the learning cycle was complete as they now became teachers of what they had been taught.

CASE SUMMARY

Maturity—self-extension, self-objectification, and a unifying philosophy of life—applies to intellectual as well as spiritual development. In either case, wholeness is the goal. The faith in Jesus of Cleopas and his friend was contaminated with doubt because of their grief. Jesus' first task was to get them to *extend* themselves by introducing long-range facts for short-term feelings. Then he had to help them *objectify* their knowledge by showing them the relationship between scriptural prophecy and his Resurrection. Once these goals were achieved, he could reveal himself as the living Christ with the power to *unify* their lives. The men of Emmaus were made whole because Jesus helped them *extend* themselves, *understand* themselves, and then *give* themselves to him as a person.

TEACHING BY SYMBOL

A curious contradiction exists between Jesus' teaching of the men of Emmaus and his counseling with the woman at the well. She was untutored, and yet Jesus led her to understand some of his heaviest theological concepts. His tact with the men on the Emmaus road was equally unexpected. As disciples of Jesus, one would expect them to remember the promise of the Resurrection with just a jog of the memory. Instead, he walked them through an elementary process and brought them to understanding with a symbol that even a child could understand. Like the scholar-ruler Nicodemus, perhaps it is the religiously sophisticated who need to relearn the basics through symbols while the simple, unclogged sinner may be ready for advanced thinking.

Christianity has always been rich in symbols, not only as a sign of recognition among exiles, but as teaching tools for children. During my college days, I remember the impression a professor made on me when he reported a study that showed that Roman Catholic students remained more faithful to their religion than either their Protestant or Jewish counterparts. One factor behind their loyalty was the meaningful role they experienced as children during mass. Even though the service was in Latin, they were active participants through the symbols of counting beads, kneeling to pray, making the sign of the cross, lighting the candles, and partaking of the cup.

Protestants rely on the written and spoken word. Reacting against the empty symbols of the Roman church, we have substituted the overkill of religious jargon. In his book *The Educational Mission of the Church,* Robert Havighurst repeats a delightful story that makes you choke on your chuckle.[1]

Bill was a thirteen-year-old boy with a shock of red hair and one eye, due to a childhood accident. He lived with his widowed mother and tolerated school. One day, his teacher invited the parents to school to witness a test of the students' spiritual I.Q. A prize of five dollars was offered for the boy or girl who did the best.

Not wanting to be embarrassed, Bill did not tell his mother about the invitation. On the day of the test, he overslept, complained of a stomach ache, and was finally pushed out of the house with instructions to bring home a loaf of bread after school. Dawdling on his way, Bill figured that he could kill more time if he bought the bread before rather than after school.

His plans went awry. As he sneaked into the classroom, the teacher said, "Bill, you've arrived just in time for the test." She held up one finger; Bill held up two fingers. She held up three fingers; Bill held up his fist. She picked up an apple from her desk; Bill held up his loaf of bread.

Surprised, the teacher announced that Bill had won the five-dollar prize. Sending the students out to recess, she then explained that the test was on insight into religious symbolism.

"I started with one finger, signifying the deity. William held up two fingers to show that there are two in the Godhead, Father and Son. I showed three fingers to signify the third element, the Holy Ghost. William held up his closed hand to show that they are the three in one. I held up the apple as the symbol of man's fall from grace, and William held up the loaf of bread, which is the bread of life, the saving grace of God. So you see what remarkable understanding the boy has."

When Bill arrived home, he showed his mother the five dollars he had won. Alarmed, she asked him how he got it.

"Well, it was this way," Bill said. "When I got there, the teacher said that I had to take this test. She held up one finger to show that I had only one eye. I held up two fingers to show that my one eye was as good as her two. She held up three fingers to show that we had only three eyes between us. I shook my fist to show what I would do to her if she didn't quit that kind of business. She picked up the apple to throw at me. I held up my loaf of bread to protect myself, and she gave me the five dollar bill to lay off."

The fiction does not belie the fact. Teaching by symbols —whether words or objects—is a dull tool in the kit of Christian education. Our failure is compounded by a secular society that has been characterized as a land of broken symbols. Rather than backing away from symbolic teaching, we should take our cue from the graffiti, pendants, and posters of the young. If the church has lost its symbols and society has broken them, the new generation will create its own. Jesus' use of broken bread to open the eyes of the men of Emmaus should arouse the interest of every teacher who has insight and integration as goals for the learning process.

JESUS' PRINCIPLES OF TEACHING AND LEARNING

Practical knowledge of educational theory made Jesus a master teacher. As with his counseling, he taught instinctively, individually, and situationally; yet there is a discernible pattern at work in his encounter with the men of Emmaus. Some of the principles are so basic to learning theory that they appear a recitation of the obvious. Others, however, are so creative that they make the current innovations in education look like historical reruns. If Jesus had a

theory of learning that could be induced from his walk and
visit with the men of Emmaus, it would include these working principles:

1. *Open communication* in a human relationship is the
   most conducive climate for learning.
2. *Total motivation* to meet a "felt need" is the highest
   level of readiness for learning.
3. *Personal trust and authoritative knowledge* earn the
   right for a teacher to participate in the learning process.
4. *Open-ended questions* encourage a student to respond
   with both facts and feelings.
5. *Fact-feeling ambivalence* is a necessary response in learning, particularly when negative feelings are involved.
6. *Erratic learning progress* requires patient and repetitive
   teaching.
7. *A fact perspective* creates intellectual insight only after
   feelings have been absorbed into an inductive process.
8. *Symbols of common experience* integrate facts and feelings into meaningful learning for the total personality.
9. *Teaching feedback* evaluates a teacher's skill in the
   learning process, that is, stimulating motivation, insight,
   and integration.
10. *Learning feedback* evaluates a student's ability to apply
    learning outcomes, that is, implementing knowledge and
    teaching others in new situations.

Jesus, the teacher, has given us a learning experience on
the Emmaus road that must be repeated again and again in
homes, churches, and schools. Our task is to communicate
truth through relationships of trust until hearts and minds
are glowing under the enthusiasm of teaching and the
authority of truth. Then in a moment of insightful encounter,
the Person of Jesus Christ must again be presented through
the symbol of the broken loaf.

Chapter Ten

HIS MINISTRY

.

BY HIS OWN definition, Jesus was first of all a minister. He said, "The Son of Man has not come to be served but to serve, and to give his life to set many others free" (Matt. 20:28).

Volumes have been written about the preaching and teaching of Jesus. Little has been said, however, about his ministerial role in relationship to his maturity. As a man who had developed self-discipline, self-confidence, and a singleness of purpose, Jesus set wide boundaries and patient time-lines for people who were changing and growing, but when he applied the same expectations to himself, he was tough. Within the context of his calling and the anointing by the Spirit of God, Jesus worked as a *goal-directed, versatile, self-starting,* and *efficient* minister who could not be destroyed by either success or disappointment.

MISSION BY OBJECTIVE

In his inaugural address, Jesus announced his mission as a fulfillment of Isaiah's prophecy:

> The Spirit of the Lord is upon me,
> Because he anointed me to preach
> good tidings to the poor:
> He hath sent me to proclaim release
> to the captives,
> And recovering of sight to the blind,
> To set at liberty them that are bruised,
> To proclaim the acceptable year of the Lord.
> (Luke 4:18–19)

Behind the romance of poetry and prophecy is a hard-nosed, realistic statement of Jesus' *mission by objective.*

Administrative theory stresses the importance of managing by objective in order to get results. Market needs are researched, profit goals are projected, human resources are engaged, and efficient techniques are employed to produce the product. After the work cycle is completed, outcomes are evaluated according to the "bottom line" objective. If the results fall short, either the goal or the process is changed.

To some, the analogy might be offensive, but Jesus set a similar process in motion when he publicly advanced the objectives of his ministerial mission. He put his *motive* on the line when he said, "The Spirit of the Lord is upon me." He declared preaching as the *means* he would employ. He defined his *market* as the poor, captive, blind, and bruised, and then, with a final stroke of daring, he predicted that the *results* would be "good tidings . . . release . . . recovered sight . . . and liberty."

Jesus knew that the anointing of the Spirit was not enough. He also had to accept the accountability for the means, the market, and the results of his ministry. Therefore, in his keynote message he brought the clarity of his objectives together with the quality of his life and the power of his calling. The standard for ministerial credentials has not changed.

A BALANCE OF STYLE

Gospel writers gave almost equal space to the preaching, teaching, counseling, and healing ministries of Jesus. Balance was evident in the time that he spent with crowds, disciples, individuals, and by himself. He was a man of ideas as well as action.

Jesus' versatility is another indicator of his maturity. A singleness of purpose did not mean fixation on a single style. He varied his approaches to keep *vitality* in his work. Certainly, his changing pace had a self-renewing quality that explains why he told his disciples who found him with the Samaritan woman, "I have food to eat that you know nothing about" (John 4:32).

Each ministry of Jesus—preaching, teaching, counseling, and healing—seems to draw strength from the other. For instance, the healing of the epileptic boy led to a closed seminar with the disciples; Jesus' sermon in the synagogue produced a debate with the scribes; and his counseling with the rich young ruler prompted a parable on the danger of riches. As his balanced style renewed his spirit, his complementary ministries increased his *authority*. Jesus could soar in the realm of ideas and yet drive home the truth with a pragmatic hammer. Because he lived on the raw edge of human need, his proclamation of truth always had a personal touch in which men and women saw themselves. In contrast to the pedantic utterances of the scribes and Pharisees, Jesus gained added vitality and authority from his versatility. No wonder the people marveled, "No man ever spoke like that" (John 7: 46).

PERSONAL INITIATIVE

Jesus was a *self-starting* man. He said, "It was the lost that the Son of Man came to seek—and to save" (Luke 19:10). Not enough weight is given to the initiative of Jesus in *seeking* the lost and *going* to the House of Israel. A pastor's study would have been too confining for him. To fulfill his mission, Jesus took what Paul Johnson has called the *"geographical initiative."* [1] He traveled the land of Palestine at least three times in order to make himself available to the poor, the broken-hearted, the captive, the blind, and the bruised. As he moved, his geographical initiative was matched by his *psychological initiative.* News of his compassion preceded him so that people sought him out.

Early in his ministry, he made his initiative for compassion known. A leper came to him and said, "If you want to, you can make me clean." Jesus, moved with compassion, put out his hand, touched the man, and cried, "Of course I want to. Be clean!" By reaching out and touching the leper, Jesus recklessly demonstrated the initiative of love. Then, to reinforce the point, he said, "Of course I want to. Be clean" (Matt. 8:2–3). Jesus may have been accentuating the obvious, but he did it to set the tone for his whole ministry.

As the news of Jesus' availability and compassion spread throughout Palestine, people in need began to come to him. Only once did he turn someone down. When the woman of Cana called out for mercy and the healing of her daughter, Jesus answered that his mission was limited to the lost sheep of Israel. However, the woman's quick rejoinder that even dogs get the crumbs from the king's table stirred his compassion so that he stretched the boundaries of his ministry to heal her daughter.

Through his preaching and teaching, Jesus kept a *spiritual initiative* as well. He extended the Law from its letter to its spirit; he challenged the Sabbath rules when his disciples were hungry; and he kept religious scholars on the defensive by pointing out the conflicts of their tradition. Still, there was not a trace of arrogance when he took the offensive. He was available without being political; he was compassionate without being sentimental; and he was aggressive without being judgmental. Unlike most people, his initiative grew out of his sense of mission rather than out of his personal ambition. He took the offensive to minister to people, not to save himself.

Economy of Effort

Self-styled messiahs are megalomaniacs. Their sense of mission has no limitations short of conquering the world—now! At the slightest signal that their efforts are being frustrated, they respond with rage and vengeance.

Jesus had a world view without sickness. His claim to be the Messiah was attested by the maturity of his response to the limited *purpose* of his ministry. The Sermon on the Mount, for instance, was used to define his relationship to the Law. He said, "You must not think that I have come to abolish the Law or the Prophets; I have not come to abolish them but to complete them" (Matt. 5:17). In a related context, he drew the limitations on his own work when he told his disciples, "By myself I can do nothing. As I hear, I judge, and my judgment is true because I do not live to please myself but to do the will of the Father who sent me" (John 5:30). Later on, he would have to test the meaning of that limitation in the garden when he faced the unknown and could only pray, "Thy will be done" (Matt. 26:42, KJV).

Jesus recognized the restrictions of *timing* on his work. Regarding the time for the coming of the Son of Man, he said that only the Father knew the answer (see Matt. 24:36). Also,

he accepted a time schedule for revealing himself that ran
contrary to popular support when he declared on several
occasions, "It is not yet the right time for me" (John 7:6).
A limitation like this, however, multiplies the meaning of
that moment when Jesus said, "It was for this very purpose
that I came to this hour. 'Father, honor your own name'"
(John 12:27–28). He knew that the purpose of his life could
not be accomplished prematurely.

The will and the timing of the Father were the general
guidelines for Jesus' ministry, but he also set some specific
limits for his work. He declared his intention to seek only
the lost of the House of Israel and thereby did not preach to
the Gentiles. Then he pulled in the circle of his influence
even tighter when he said, "It is not the healthy who need
the doctor, but those who are ill. I have not come to invite
the 'righteous' but the 'sinners'—to change their ways" (Luke
5:32). To reach Jews who were sinners, he risked eating and
drinking with them. With each deliberate choice, criticism
mounted, but Jesus knew he could not be all things to all
men and still accomplish his chosen task.

Jesus was not a man for all situations. When he went home
to Nazareth, he encountered the contempt of familiarity.
His family and his friends knew him too well to believe that
he could perform miracles. Rejection at home speaks, not
only to the commonness of his early life, but also to the fullness of his humanity. Surely Jesus expected a different re-
ception; so it must have been with sadness that he called out
the truth, "No prophet goes unhonored—except in his native town or with his own relations or in his own home"
(Mark 6:4).

When pressed to extend his ministry to a position on certain *social issues,* Jesus refused to be diverted from his primary task. The Pharisees tried to trap him into making a
pledge of allegiance to either Caesar or God, but he judi-

ciously avoided political involvement by saying, "Then give to Caesar . . . what belongs to Caesar and to God what belongs to God!" (Matt. 22:21).

In another instance, a man asked Jesus to settle a *personal dispute* with his brother over the family inheritance. Jesus again defined himself out of the situation:

> "My dear man, who appointed me a judge or arbitrator in your affairs?"
> And then, turning to the disciples, he said to them:
> "Notice that, and be on your guard against covetousness in any shape or form. For a man's real life in no way depends upon the number of his possessions" (Luke 12:14–15).

To explain the point further, Jesus told the parable of the rich fool. He could not afford to be turned from his spiritual mission by social or personal disputes.

No better example of Jesus' maturity exists than the limitations he placed on *emotional involvements* with the people he healed. Sick and selfish leaders need all the disciples they can get in order to bolster their ever-sagging egos. All effective healers, however, face the problems of emotional transference when the patient, client, or parishioner redirects feelings of hostility or love to the person who guides the healing process. Healing is not complete until this dependence line is broken and the person is also emotionally free. Independence is the final goal of healing.

Jesus showed his strength at this point after he had healed the psychotic man of Gadarenes. Naturally, the grateful man wanted to be a disciple of Jesus. Most healers would have been quick to take his offer so that they could have instant proof of their power with such a miraculous exhibit. From experience Jesus knew that the man's growth potential would be curtailed by this dependence. Eventually he would become psychologically and spiritually retarded. Therefore, he told him, "Go home to your own people, . . . and tell them what the Lord has done for you, and how kind he has been to you" (Mark 5:19). By drawing the limits of emotional dependence, Jesus set the man fully free.

All the limitations that Jesus accepted for his ministry— purpose, timing, place, and situation—served to focus his energies on his most essential tasks. An *economy of effort* was partially responsible for the amazing achievements we attribute to his short life. If we assume he was effective just because he was the Son of God, we have an excuse for our own ineffectiveness; but if the quality of his performance was also related to the maturity that let him put limits on his efforts, Jesus, the Son of Man, has taught us something about improving the effectiveness of our own work.

THE COURAGE OF IMPERFECTION

Jesus' ministry was not an unqualified success. If his key-note sermon in the synagogue is used to evaluate the results of his work, no one would dispute the fact that he preached the gospel to the poor, healed the broken-hearted, delivered the captives, brought sight to the blind, and gave liberty to the bruised. In fact, when he appraised his ministry in prayer with his Father, he reported, "I have brought you honor upon earth, I have completed the task which you gave me to do" (John 17:4).

When it came to individual situations, there were exceptions. He told the Father. "As long as I was with them, I kept them by the power that you gave me; I guarded them, and not one of them was destroyed, except the son of destruction—that the scripture might come true" (John 17:12). Although there is the sound of the inevitable in these words, scriptural evidence points to the fact that Jesus did not take his disappointments lightly. Certainly he must have been hurt when he was rejected by his family and friends in Nazareth so that "he could do nothing miraculous there" (Mark 6:5).

The depth of Jesus' disappointment was shown when he failed to convince the rich young ruler that eternal life was worth more than possessions. Jesus looked at him and loved him; so when the young man turned away sadly, the loss was mutual. There was even greater sadness when Jesus realized that he had not won Jerusalem. He wept:

> "O Jerusalem, Jerusalem, you murder the prophets and stone the messengers that are sent to you! How often have I longed to gather your children round me like a bird gathering her brood together under her wings, but you would never have it" (Luke 13:34).

Whether with an individual or a city, Jesus suffered when he failed.

According to contemporary standards for instant success, Jesus also failed with Peter. Jesus went to the cross with the words of betrayal still ringing in his ears. Furthermore, on the cross he had no final assurance that his own mission was a success because his last prayer, "My God, my God, why did you forsake me?" (Mark 15:34), was a question that went unanswered. Ambiguity is a form of failure for most people.

How, then, can Jesus claim to have finished his work? The answer is that his sense of mission and his personal maturity gave him what Rollo May has called "the courage of imperfection." [2] In testimony to his wholeness, Jesus could admit defeat without losing the perspective of his total mission or the integrity of his self-concept. May, in his book *Power and Innocence*, contends that the malaise behind our national despair is the loss of the "sense of the tragic." When a nation or a person cannot admit failure, the brittle façade of success will shatter and become despair in the face of reality.

In his early struggles for maturity, Jesus had learned to

defer immediate gratification for long-range goals, to live
with his own limitations, and to recognize that the whole of
life was greater than the sum of the parts. The "courage of
imperfection" is the crowning proof that Jesus was a real,
complete, and mature man.

A MESSAGE FOR MINISTERS

Ministerial drop-outs are decimating the ranks of the
clergy. Perhaps the wrong ministerial model is being used.
Overgeneralized objectives, overspecialized functions, over-
extended boundaries, and overglamourized expectations will
produce fatigue in any profession.

Nothing about the future promises relief. Andrew Greeley,
in his book *Religion in the Year Two Thousand,* does not
foresee the demise of religion but predicts increasing secular
pressure.[3] As the society becomes more pluralistic, for example, hostility will develop against Christian values that have
been dominant in the past. Individuals will not be able to
hide behind institutional positions on ethical issues. The process of dehumanization will continue so that Christianity
will have to speak more directly to the dilemmas of life,
death, and sex than it has in the past. Ministers will continue
to be caught in the storm.

Using the Model of Jesus as an antidote to fatigue, a minister might rebuild the meaning of his or her vocation by asking the following questions:

1. Have I stated specific objectives, means, market, and
   results for my ministry?
2. Have I developed the versatility of style that will give
   my ministry vitality and authority?
3. Have I taken the initiative to minister on the "growing
   edge" of human need?
4. Have I accepted my limitations of purpose, time, place,

and situation in order to concentrate on strategic tasks?

5. Have I submitted myself before God for an honest appraisal of my effectiveness in meeting the goals of my mission?

6. Have I learned to accept disappointment in the perspective of God's will and my total ministry?

Affirmative answers to these questions are not possible unless a minister is moving toward what Paul called "the goal of true [personal and spiritual] maturity" (Rom. 12:2). Then, with the anointing of the Spirit of the Lord, Jesus' promise to his disciples can be claimed by those who are called to serve today. As Jesus looked back on the results of his ministry and then ahead to those who would follow him, he predicted, "The man who believes in me . . . will do even greater things than these" (John 14:12). The promise has never been canceled.

Part Five

THE ANSWER

"I have given you . . . an example
so that you may do as I have done."
John 13:15

Chapter Eleven

JESUS, OUR MODEL

A FAST-MOVING, superindustrial society has placed unprecedented strain upon human personality and interpersonal relationships. Each leap forward seems to have its trade-off with another delicate piece of personal integrity. Technology takes the brunt of the blame by breeding new generations of machines that are superior substitutes, not only for the strength of hands, arms, and legs, but often for the senses of eyes, ears, and mind. Whatever the machine—a "fail-safe" missile system that can set fire to our earth or a household robot that can babysit our children—we are not quite sure whether we are masters or slaves. Like the worn-down joke about the jetliner flown by a computer, "Everything is under control . . . under control . . . under control . . ."

Behind the mixed blessings of technology lurk other invaders into the sovereign domain of human personality. Research continues to march across the "no-man's land" of genetics with guerrilla raids into the darker side of the brain. Again, on that battlefield, we cannot sort out friends and enemies by the color of their hats. Minimal comfort is gained from the assurances of scientists that moral codes and ethics committees stand guard at the outposts of our individuality. Just one revelation of experimental abuse shatters our confidence once again.

Dizzy from dodging under the Sword of Damocles which dangles on a fraying thread above our heads, we cast a desperate eye toward some freedom-saving, security-producing authority. Traditional institutions, such as the home and the church, are too much like us—slowly picking the way across a moral bog by gingerly testing every clump before shifting full weight to a new position. Meantime, the natural momentum of security speeds us on toward a centralized power which can save as well as protect us. Selectively and selfishly, we feed the voracious appetite of government by lobbying for benefits which advance our security while protesting the ensuing regulations which curtail our freedom. Bureaucracy that is more powerful than our policies becomes a compatriot with machines that are quicker-than-the-eye, and with research that is more advanced than our ethics. Sooner or later, a common predisposition to paranoia is uncovered when the elbow of someone else's freedom gouges into the ribs of our security. Contrary to popular belief, the rights of human personality and the privileges of interpersonal relationships must be protected by public regulation when the values of personal responsibility lag behind the need of the times, or lack the power of social consensus.

Wounded and cornered, our collective humanity strikes out blindly in all directions at once. Crime in the streets, protest on the mall, catharsis on the couch, chants in the cult, and even the popularity of being "born again," have at least one thing in common—our personal search for identity, independence, and integrity.

One good outcome of our stress and search is the honing of our sensitivity toward the meaning of persons and the principles of human relationships. Whether home, church, school, business or government, the social institution which most effectively addresses these questions is the institution to which we turn. Likewise, the discipline of study whose research and theory firms up the footing for personal wholeness and interpersonal well-being moves to the forefront of interest and influence.

By self-definition, psychology is the field of study with a particular responsibility for understanding human nature from its genetic origins to its last rational gasp. Through its theorists and practitioners, psychology has spoken to the wide range of personal issues—usually with scientific modesty, but sometimes with philosophical arrogance. All too often, the hidden premise at both extremes is a humanistic, reductionistic, and behavioristic view of personality. Thus, when the theory is popularized in practice as a technique for growth or therapy for healing, the subtle assumptions behind the practice are not readily apparent to a general public that only knows the aching need for some answers to the human dilemma.

Projected into the future, psychological theories about human nature will gain awesome power. In the company of biological, chemical, social and ecological studies of personality and behavior, psychology will operate in an ever-widening sphere of influence. Reinforcing its expanded power will be the continuing sophistication of machines, the mind-boggling discoveries of advanced research, and the pervasive dominance of government. More and more, people will grasp at straws which promise even the most fragile holds on human destiny—whether in violence or peace, fantasy or

reality, sensuality or spirituality, chaos or community. Debate
over the questions of whether or not psychologists should
take value positions will no longer be academic. Anyone who
researches, teaches, or practices the principles of personality
is a value-maker with responsibility to consider the consequences that ensue in human behavior.

Christians, now and in the future, are particularly vulnerable to popular trends in psychological theory and practice.
Because our faith is centered in the nature of a Person, activated in the changing of human nature, and demonstrated
in the quality of interpersonal relationships, we are open to
entertain any ideas or aids which complement our desire to
change and grow. Advertisers, publishers, and producers have
already exploited the ready market of Christian interest in
everything from psychological best-sellers to prime-time spe-
cials on psychologized religion. Without the philosophical
sophistication to critique the premises about personality, or
without a working model against which to judge the applied
principles of psychology, Christians are easily split between
open-mouthed gullibility and closed-minded rejection. In
between are those who do a balancing act with their faith
and their knowledge, holding in one hand biblical truth
about human nature, and in the other, contradictory psychological theories about personality. To avoid the confrontation required by intellectual integrity, they adapt to
the process of keeping one hand closed whenever the other is
open until it becomes as automatic as a jerk of the knee or
a wink of the eye.

Our alternative is to have a biblical view of personality and
human relationships—one that is sound in theory and workable in practice. Not that psychology should become a closed
book for Christians, but that both secular and religious ventures into personality theory and practice should be subject
to the confrontation of open debate, the integration of com-

mon truth, and the investigation of the areas that remain unreconciled and unknown.

My premise is that the life history of Jesus gives us a rational, workable, and meaningful standard to confront, integrate, and investigate the relationships between Christian faith and psychological theory. More than that, I assert that the human development of Jesus is inseparable from his divine essence in the Christian faith. Above all, I posit that the personality and practice of Jesus give us a personal Model for our own development.

For most of us, this is virgin territory. Simple faith permits us to reach out and embrace Jesus, the Son of God, as Lord and Redeemer; but to follow him at the same time, as the fully human Son of Man, may require a more advanced faith than we can muster. If so, the urgency of our need to recapture the meaning of persons against the floodtide of impersonal forces may rescue us. Rising above a superfaith which mystically overextends the claims of Jesus as the Son of God, and above the subfaith which skeptically refuses to go beyond the claims of Jesus as the Son of Man, we come to the pinnacle of the biblical perspective. Here, like all eternal truth, is the paradox which holds Jesus as Son of Man and Son of God in creative and harmonious tension. Uneasy though we may be at this point, no other faith is radical enough or mature enough to live with the mystery of the Incarnation and learn the meaning of Jesus, our Model.

Thus, I present again the premises which identify Jesus as the Son of Man, our Model. As a standard for debating assumptions about personality theory and critiquing the practice of psychologized religion, these premises are just a starting point. Theologically, they represent the search for biblical facts on the human side of the Incarnation and, therefore, provide additional balance on the creedal scale of Christian faith. But for our primary purpose and in response to the urgency of our personal needs, I present Jesus as our Model by whom we measure our own development as human beings created in the image of God and as disciples of the One who became flesh and lived among us.

Jesus is our Model of a real and complete man. Fully human as well as fully divine, Jesus experienced human birth and growth with all the attendant problems and promises. As a person, he exhibited the full range of human needs, motives, and emotions. If described by the clustering of his personality traits, Jesus was a retiring, sensitive, and inner-directed man, but not without the capability of strong responses and surprise reactions. In fact, we see ourselves in him, with the exception that he alone had the record of unblemished integrity despite total temptation. A real and complete man, Jesus had to live with his humanity as we have to live with ours.

Jesus is our Model of the mature person. He had the natural and legitimate will to *live* (self-preservation), will to *be* (self-actualization), and the will to be *whole* (self-integrity). In the temptation, Satan tried to turn each of these human needs to sin. Jesus had the choice of directing their powerful energies either by his own will or by the will of God. Not without struggle, he chose the mission that God had given him.

Maturity was the reward. Jesus became a self-extensive person who could defer the immediate need to gratify physical drives for the sake of higher and longer-term spiritual goals. He was also a self-objectifying person who was confident in his strengths and realistic about his limitations. Furthermore, he had a unifying philosophy of life that met his need for self-integrity. The will of the Father was the "center of the center" for all aspects of his humanity. Through temptation, Jesus personalized the meaning of maturity for us.

Jesus is our Model of a disciplined character. No special

gift or power was given to Jesus to resist temptation or achieve maturity. Throughout his life, he had to cultivate the disciplines of prayer, Scripture, and obedience. Without these tools for self-mastery, he could not remain free from sin, develop his potential as a person, or fulfill his mission.

Prayer was a habit and an attitude with Jesus. Publicly and privately, he maintained fellowship with the Father—giving thanks, seeking guidance, and restoring energy. As a discipline, however, Jesus used prayer as a means to keep his human needs within the perspective of God's will as he confronted new situations. Prayer was Jesus' proof that maturity is not instantaneous.

To complement the inner discipline of prayer, Jesus schooled himself in the Scriptures. From them he gained the authority for his preaching, teaching, and healing ministries. Having rejected the tradition of the scribes and Pharisees, Jesus risked his credibility on the evidence that the Scriptures were the inspired, accurate, and permanent Word of God. He also claimed that his words had the full authority of Revealed Truth. As such, he unveiled the value of the Scriptures as an instrument for personal pruning, a standard for self-judgment, and the source of eternal life. Extended outwardly, then, Jesus put a premium on the discipline of scriptural knowledge by using it as the single authority against the forces of evil during his temptation.

Both prayer and scriptural knowledge imply obedience, a discipline in its own right. Jesus had to learn to obey through suffering in order to fulfill his human potential and his redemptive mission. Three levels of self-denial are built into the discipline of obedience in Jesus' life. At the lowest level, Jesus obeyed when he put spiritual values over his own physical needs. Later he was asked to obey by a ministry in which the needs of others took precedence over his self-interest. All this was preparation for the final act when he was asked to obey God's will and die rather than save himself.

By example, he taught us that when obedience is a discipline
of love, the benefits are a personal relationship with the Father, understanding of the Son's words, and the "presence-in-
residence" of the Holy Spirit.

Jesus is our Model for understanding people. As a direct
outgrowth of his own experience, Jesus taught certain principles about persons that represent his working theory of
human personality. In response to the implied question,
Who is a person? Jesus enunciated the principle that an individual is infinitely valuable, uniquely different, and in-
separably one. Logically, the next question was, How then
does a person change and grow? Jesus taught that the quality
of life was determined by the motivations of the inner person. Through the insight of truth, one can change and grow
toward maturity. Insight, however, does not guarantee
change. Another question must be asked: How is a person
made whole? With an experiential grasp on theology and
psychology, Jesus said that integration was the result of making God's will the unifying center for every motive and action of body, mind, and soul.

Jesus is our Model for working with people. In his ministry, Jesus spent as much time practicing the principles of
personhood as he did teaching them. As a *counselor* with the
Samaritan woman at the well, he demonstrated the process
of healing: (1) His *love* accepted her as a person; (2) his
maturity exposed her need; (3) his *authority* drew out her
guilt; (4) his *integrity* provided a basis for hope; and (5)
his *person* became the focus for her salvation. As always, Jesus left the final decision to the woman herself.

With the men of Emmaus, Jesus served as a *teacher.*
After being accepted as a walking companion, he created a
climate of trust by asking open-ended questions to which the
men could respond with both facts and feelings. Recognizing
their ambivalence, Jesus gave a lecture in which he brought
scriptural facts into a synergic view of his life, death, and

Resurrection. A sense of history turned their despair into hope.

With the skill of a master teacher, Jesus then let the students take the initiative. They invited him to dinner where he could communicate privileged information through the symbol of his death—the breaking of the bread. The experience that they had denied was now reintroduced into their consciousness. Immediately, their eyes were open, and they saw the proof of his living presence in the symbol of his death.

Teaching and learning feedback followed for Jesus and the Emmaean men. Jesus' competence as a teacher was attested by his sensitivity in entering at the level of the students' needs and by his skill in firing their motivation for insightful self-learning. In turn, the men of Emmaus produced evidence of learning change by running to Jerusalem to share their new knowledge with the backing of logical proof and personal conviction.

Jesus, the *minister,* rigorously applied the principles of personhood to himself when he set the expectations for his work with people. In his keynote sermon, he announced the anointing of the Spirit as his *motive,* preaching as his *means;* the poor, captive, blind, and bruised as his *market;* and "good tidings . . . release . . . recovered sight . . . and liberty" (Luke 4:18) as his *results.* To implement his mission by objective, Jesus utilized a *balanced style* of preaching, teaching, and healing so that he could meet a variety of needs, retain his vitality, and build complementary strengths into his ministry. Never lapsing into a defensive mood, he took the geographical, psychological, and spiritual *initiative* to serve on the critical edge of human need.

An *economy of effort* also characterized the ministry of Jesus. To fulfill his mission, he set specific performance targets for his work and accepted the limitations of purpose, time, place, and situation in order to give strategic focus to his energies. From the perspective of these guidelines, Jesus could live with ambiguity and accept disappointments because he never lost sight of his identity or his purpose.

Jesus is our Model for a whole life. A study of Jesus necessarily concludes with his call for wholeness—a dynamic of both command and promise. Under the directive, "Thou shalt love the Lord thy God with all thy heart, and with all thy soul and with all thy mind" (Matt. 22:37), Jesus asked that we submit our *self-consciousness* to the consciousness of God as an act of love. Our renewed *self-concept* then must be worked out in human relationships according to the corollary charge, "Thou shalt love thy neighbor as thyself" (Matt. 22:39). Wholeness leaves no dimension of personality untouched—vertical and horizontal, central and pervasive.

Jesus' promises exceed his demands. By obeying his own commandments, he could recommend the qualities of wholeness from experience. *Fullness of life* is a promise that opens up an unexplored range of human potential and permits a person to be "creatively present" in the task or situation of the moment. *Freedom* to live "inside out" is a realistic hope for one liberated from baser desires and inner conflict by the insight of truth in Christ. *Joy,* uniquely defined as the kind that Jesus knew, follows freedom. Never sought as an end in itself, his joy was the tracing of obedient love. Whether in "being" or "doing," Jesus found meaning and satisfaction— the essence of joy and a quality of wholeness.

As the capstone of his promises, Jesus willed his *peace* to us as a mark of separation from the secular world. His peace is not an armed truce for a civil war within a person; it is the full surrender of self-consciousness to the mind and consciousness of Christ. Without presuming that the struggle to grow comes to an end or that external pressures diminish, we find that peace is the assurance that, through the experience and example of Jesus, we can still learn the meaning of those hard but hope-filled words:

Here and now we *are* God's children. We don't know what we shall become in the future. We only know that, if reality were to break through, we should reflect his likeness, for we should see him as he really is (1 John 3:2).

NOTES

Chapter 1

1. Philip Vollmer, *The Modern Student's Life of Christ* (New York: Fleming H. Revell, 1912), p. 343.

2. Ibid., p. 341.

3. Thomas J. J. Altizer, *The Gospel of Christian Atheism* (Philadelphia: Westminster Press, 1966), p. 136.

4. Walter E. Bundy, *The Psychic Health of Jesus* (New York: Macmillan, 1922), p. 27.

5. Ibid., p. 92.

6. Hugh J. Schonfield, *The Passover Plot: New Light on the History of Jesus* (New York: D. Geiss Associates, dist. by Random House, 1965); *The Jesus Party* (New York: Macmillan, 1974).

7. Albert Schweitzer, *The Psychiatric Study of Jesus* (Boston: Beacon Press, 1948), p. 5.

8. Sigmund Freud, *Moses and Monotheism: Three Essays* (New York: Alfred A. Knopf, 1939).

9. Erik Erikson, *The Young Man Luther: A Study in Psychoanalysis and History* (New York: W. W. Norton, 1958).

10. Erik Erikson, *Gandhi's Truth—On the Origins of Militant Non-violence* (New York: W. W. Norton, 1969).

11. Sigmund Freud and W. C. Bullitt, *Thomas Woodrow Wilson: A Psychoanalytic Psychological Study* (Boston: Houghton Mifflin, 1966).

12. C. S. Lewis, *Surprised by Joy* (New York: Harcourt, Brace & Co., 1955), p. 191.

Chapter 3

1. R. B. Cattell, "Principal Trait Clusters for Describing Personality," *Psychological Bulletin*, No. 42, 1945, pp. 129–61.
2. David Riesman, *The Lonely Crowd* (Garden City: Doubleday Anchor Books, 1953).

Chapter 4

1. Robert Jay Lifton, *Explorations in Psychohistory* (New York: Simon & Schuster, 1975).
2. John R. Hersey, *Here to Stay* (New York: Alfred A. Knopf, 1963).
3. C. S. Lewis, *Surprised by Joy* (New York: Harcourt, Brace & Co., 1955), p. 226.
4. Gordon W. Allport, *Personality: A Psychological Interpretation* (New York: Henry Holt & Co., 1937), pp. 213 ff.
5. Ibid., p. 217
6. Ibid., p. 214.
7. C. S. Lewis, *God in the Dock* (Grand Rapids: Wm. B. Eerdmans, 1970), p. 58.
8. Gordon W. Allport, *The Individual and His Religion* (New York: Macmillan, 1950), p. 57.
9. Ibid., p. 72.
10. Elton Trueblood, *A Place to Stand* (New York: Harper & Row, 1969), p. 60.

Chapter 6

1. Karl Menninger, *Whatever Became of Sin?* (New York: Hawthorn Books, 1973), p. 228.
2. Charles F. Kemp, *Physicians of the Soul* (New York: Macmillan, 1947), p. 17.
3. Alexander Bruce, *The Parabolic Teaching of Christ* (New York: George H. Boran, 1886), p. 25.

4. Ibid., p. 27.
5. Os Guinness, *In Two Minds* (Downers Grove: Intervarsity Press, 1976).
6. Alvin Toffler, *Future Shock* (New York: Random House, 1970), p. 95.

Chapter 7

1. Bruce Larson, *The Relational Revolution* (Waco, Tex.: Word Books, 1976), p. 87.
2. C. S. Lewis, *The Great Divorce* (London: Geoffrey Bles, 1945).
3. Larson, *Relational Revolution*, p. 93.
4. Norman Cousins, "Winston Churchill and the Human Spirit," *Saturday Review*, 6 February 1965, p. 18.
5. Jean-François Revel, *Without Marx or Jesus* (Garden City: Doubleday, 1970).
6. C. S. Lewis, *Surprised by Joy* (New York: Harcourt, Brace & Co., 1955), p. 219.
7. Ibid., p. 238.
8. Thomas à Kempis, *The Imitation of Christ* (New York: Macmillan, 1918), p. 236.
9. Norman Mailer, "The Search for Carter," *New York Times Magazine*, 26 September 1976, p. 20.

Chapter 9

1. Robert J. Havighurst, *The Educational Mission of the Church* (Philadelphia: Westminster Press, 1965), pp. 39–41.

Chapter 10

1. Paul Johnson, *Psychology of Pastoral Care* (New York: Abingdon-Cokesbury Press, 1953), p. 82.
2. Rollo May, *The Art of Counseling* (New York: Abingdon-Cokesbury Press, 1939), p. 177.
3. Andrew M. Greeley, *Religion in the Year Two Thousand* (Mission, Kans.: Sheed Andrews & McMeel, 1969).